SPOOKY
New Jersey

Tales of Hauntings, Strange Happenings,
and Other Local Lore

Second Edition

RETOLD BY S. E. SCHLOSSER

ILLUSTRATED BY PAUL G. HOFFMAN

Globe
Pequot

GUILFORD, CONNECTICUT

Globe
Pequot

An imprint of Rowman & Littlefield

Distributed by NATIONAL BOOK NETWORK

Text copyright © 2017 S. E. Schlosser

Illustrations copyright © 2017 Paul G. Hoffman

British Library Cataloguing in Publication Information available

Library of Congress Cataloging-in-Publication Data available

ISBN 978-1-4930-2714-9 (paperback)

ISBN 978-1-4930-2798-9 (ebook)

∞™ The paper used in this publication meets the minimum requirements of American National Standard for Information Sciences—Permanence of Paper for Printed Library Materials, ANSI/NISO Z39.48-1992.

For my family: David, Dena, Tim, Arlene, Hannah, Emma, Nathan, Ben, Deb, Gabe, Clare, Jack, and Karen.

For Anthony, Erika, and Karen, with thanks for their contribution to the book.

For Mary Norris, Mimi, Gillian, Gwen, Sarah, and the Globe Pequot staff. Thanks so much for your hard work on the Spooky series.

For Paul, who continues to amaze me with his fabulous illustrations.

For Loyd and Vernell Schlosser, who came to New Jersey in a Ford touring car and decided to stay!

And for the staff of the West Milford Diner. Thanks for all the coffee and the encouragement as I worked on Spooky New Jersey.

* * *

Contents

Spooky Sites . . .

and where to find them

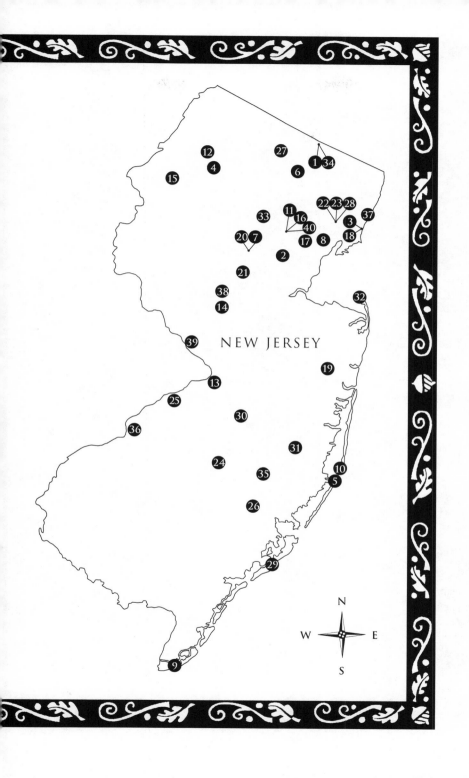

Introduction

"I was bred and born in the briar patch," Brer Rabbit once told Brer Fox, and that is me in a nutshell. I was bred and born in New Jersey, and its folklore is in my bones. I have been surrounded by stories all my life. My grandparents arrived in New Jersey separately. According to family legend, they attended the same youth group but did not "go" together until the day they both attended a church baseball game. My grandfather, who was catching, was hit in the face by a foul ball and suffered a nosebleed. My grandmother, who was a nurse, doctored him up and then spent the rest of the afternoon walking with him to "assist his recovery." Of such events is history made.

My family lore also contains some rather tall but true tales. My father, who was quite mischievous as a small boy, once had a mythic fall from the attic. He passed right through the second floor and partway through the ceiling of the first before becoming lodged. If the ceiling had been a bit less sturdy, our family lore would probably contain the ghost of my great-grandmother, who was sleeping on the living-room couch at the time. She promptly leapt to her feet and shouted "DA-VID!" at the top of her lungs. Apparently he was fairly easy to identify, even though only his bottom half was showing. (Needless to say, he got into quite a bit of trouble.) This same David actually lived to grow up, marry, and produce four children, of whom I am one. He is the person who read me stories from infancy onward, and who fostered a love of folklore within me that survives to this day.

Of course, I learned a great deal of local New Jersey lore at school. Imagine my astonishment when I heard about the Devil worshippers who used Washington Rock, a local state park near my home, for their nefarious ceremonies. I would later discover how truly spooky that park was. On the other hand, I was quite pleased to learn that a pirate's treasure trove was buried at the top of Schooley's Mountain to the north. My imagination really ran wild when I found out that the Jersey Devil haunted the Pinelands a few hours south of where I lived, and that sometimes he came north—at least that's what my friends said.

Trips to the Jersey shore included lots of sunscreen and a few tales of ghosts who roam the beaches. Too bad I didn't hear the story of Dem Bones when my family used to bathe in the sea at Sandy Hook. I would have insisted on staying overnight if it meant a chance to glimpse glowing skeletons dancing and drinking around a blazing fire. But I am glad I didn't meet the ghost of the Searcher when we stayed at Long Beach Island; I would have found it too difficult to answer her mournful questions about a long-lost love.

My meanderings through the Garden State also took me to Cape May, with its plethora of hauntings. My favorite story is that of the pretty ghost who likes to show herself to guests in the mirrors of a certain bed-and-breakfast. Farther north, I once paid a visit to Atlantic City. Something about the boardwalk at night—perhaps the whisper of the wind—reminded me strongly of the tales of the phantom ship of Captain Sandovate, doomed for eternity to roam the local waters with its crew begging for just one sip of water. Though I made no formal sighting, the night was spooky enough to send me shivering back to my hotel.

Driving through the Pinelands, I always kept a watch out for the rascally Jersey Devil, though he was rarely sighted after one spectacularly frightening week in January 1909. And moving northward through the state, I remembered the ghosts of the Aaron Burrs, father and son, who haunt Princeton University; of a little girl once seen by George Washington himself; of Joseph Bonaparte (brother of Napoleon), who haunts his old property in Bordentown; of Albert Payson Terhune, the famous collie breeder whose spirit still resides at his sister's house in Pompton Lakes; and many more.

Today I live in New York State, but only a half mile from the New Jersey border. The town of West Milford with its mysterious Clinton Road is nearby, and every once in a while—during daylight hours—I like to drive down its shadowy, twisty length, remembering tales of ghosts and witches and a famous black dog. The animal is said to guard one or more bodies buried by the Mob along this desolate stretch of road. Surely I exaggerate, you say? By no means! At least one famous murder case—that of the Iceman—was solved after a frozen body was discovered nearby.

There are a myriad of tales about New Jersey, and I could go on literally for days—just ask my friends, who usually have to buy me dinner to get me to be quiet! To me, New Jersey is not just a state seething with history and spooky stories—it is also the place where I grew up, and it is still very much my home.

—Sandy Schlosser

PART ONE
Ghost Stories

1

The Blue Lantern

RINGWOOD STATE PARK, RINGWOOD

My wife and I came to an agreement shortly after we married: I would happily accompany her on her "ghostly" ramblings as long as she chose to visit spots where both of us could pursue our various interests. This means that we mostly visit haunted state parks, which suits an outdoors fellow like me just fine. While my wife indulges her psychic self by wandering through old, well-preserved haunted houses, I hike along the various trails provided by the park systems. When she visits old graveyards, I take along my bike and explore the beautifully manicured grounds. If she takes a cruise on a mysterious lake and watches for aquatic monsters of the mythical kind, I rent a kayak and paddle along behind the boat. So far, all our outings have been enjoyable ones and have added a delightful dimension to an already happy marriage.

"So where are we off to today, Jeannie?" I asked as we climbed into our SUV. As usual, Jeannie's bag was full of maps and pamphlets and "ghost guides."

"We are headed to Ringwood State Park in Ringwood, New Jersey," my petite, red-haired wife said cheerfully. "According to the literature, the park lies in the heart of the Ramapo Mountains and is easily accessible from exit 57 off Route 287."

"You sound like a guidebook," I said with a grin as I started the engine and pulled out of the driveway. "What about the park draws us there this fine July morning?"

"Ringwood State Park consists of some of the original land and buildings of the 'once flourishing iron industry developed in 1740 by the Ringwood Company,'" Jeannie said, reading directly from a page she had printed from the Internet. Abandoning the paper, she continued from memory: "It was the home of several well-known ironmasters, including one Scottish man, Robert Erskine, who was the surveyor-general for General Washington himself. Later, it was owned by a man called Martin Ryerson, who ran the local ironworks and built the Ringwood Manor."

Her voice deepened when she mentioned the manor. I knew that tone of voice. "Don't tell me, I know!" I said teasingly. "Ringwood Manor just happens to be haunted! By who— Robert Erskine? Martin Ryerson?"

"Ringwood Manor is a Gothic Revival mansion with classical embellishments. It sits on a low hill overlooking a small pond in the midst of a beautiful valley," Jeannie said in a reproving tone, irritated that I had stolen her big revelation. "It was last owned by the wealthy Hewitt family and was donated to the state in 1936 by Erskine Hewitt. It is supposed to be haunted by the ghost of a housemaid. She can be heard moving about in a small room on the second floor. There are reports of noises coming from the empty room—footsteps, sounds of heavy objects dropping, soft crying. They say that members of the staff keep finding the bedroom door ajar and the bed rumpled."

"Only one housemaid?" I questioned. "Surely there must be more ghosts than that?"

Jeannie glared at me. She often wondered aloud how a faithful believer in ghosts could have married a skeptic like me. "They say there is an unmarked grave filled with the remains of French soldiers who fought during the Revolutionary War. After dark, you can hear soft, sad voices speaking in French. There is also the ghost of a servant named Jeremiah, and Mrs. Hewitt is said to wander around the house."

"What about my pal, Robert Erskine?" I asked. "Surely he must roam the grounds?"

"Yes, he does. Strange lights have been seen over his grave, and sometimes the bricks at the base of the tomb are found on the ground, as if they had been thrust out by some ghostly force inside," said Jeannie.

"Sounds spooky," I said. Jeannie glared at me for my flippant tone. Deciding I had teased her enough for one drive, I asked if there were any good hiking trails in this park.

Jeannie relaxed a bit, pulled out a map, and began enumerating the various attractions of the park for non-believers. The talk lasted until we came around a bend in Sloatsburg Road and turned to enter the park. On a hill ahead of us stood the fancy manor house Jeannie had described. I raised my eyebrows, impressed by its regal appearance. A large pond lay off to our left, and the smaller Mill Pond was right beside the drive. I stopped at the booth, paid a small entrance fee, and drove to the parking lot near the house.

"I'm going to take a house tour," Jeannie said as we strolled toward the park office. "Would you like to come?" It was her turn to tease me.

"No thanks!" I said. "I'm only stopping at the house long enough to get a map of the hiking trails. How long do you think the house tour will last? If it's a short one, then I'll just meander around the pond and meet you back here when you are done."

"Maybe an hour?" Jeannie guessed. "Let's ask."

The girl in the office gave me a map of the park and told Jeannie the tours lasted anywhere from forty-five minutes to an hour. I mentally added another half hour, since my wife would probably interrogate the tour guide about any reported paranormal happenings once the official tour was over. There was enough time for a short hike on one of the paths or a relaxing stroll around the grounds and down to Sally's Pond in the valley just below the house. I opted for the second option, bade my wife a fond good-bye, which she hardly heard in her raptures over the columned porch next to the driveway, and strolled off.

First things first. I spotted a cannon, a huge mortar, and a giant chain on the hillside in front of the house, facing the pond. I went to examine them, removing from my pocket some of the literature Jeannie had handed to me upon parting. The documentation identified the cannon as a deck gun from the USS *Constitution* (Old Ironsides); the huge mortar was one of two used at the siege of Vicksburg, and the chain was a replica of the huge West Point Chain, which had been forged from Ringwood iron and used to obstruct British navigation of the Hudson River. A hammer and anvil and a giant wheel shaft from the old gristmill were among the other relics at that location.

Reluctantly, I tore myself away from the equipment and wandered past the front of the house toward the side yard, which led down to the shores of Sally's Pond. I passed a glassed-in porch filled with white wicker furniture, surrounded on three sides by a brick patio guarded by a couple of red-stone sphinx and some large plants with black flowers that the bumblebees seemed to find irresistible. Personally, I thought black flowers were a bit on the grim side, but I wasn't a bee.

I stepped onto the side lawn and headed down the hill, staring in perplexity at two large, free-standing iron gates. There was no wall around them and no difference—to my eyes—between the lawn on one side versus the lawn on the other. There were not even vines to twine artistically up their ten- to twelve-foot height. Shaking my head at the vagaries of landscape artists, I strolled through the center of them and down to the pond, disturbing a family of Canada geese. Mama and Papa Goose herded their group of teenagers into the water as I passed their resting place and strolled into the shade of some truly awesome giant oak trees.

Near the edge of the pond, the view was mostly obstructed by trees and bushes growing on the bank. I continued my way around the side, hoping to find a clearer spot. A small stream meandered across the lawn, dove into a pipe under a dirt and gravel bridge, and reappeared on the far side. As I crossed the stream, a flock of birds burst out of the trees overhead, yelling crossly to one another and heading for a more interesting tree across the way.

I took a deep breath of the summer air, at peace with the world. This was a truly lovely spot. A dirt road was coming to meet me from the hillside to my right. *Ah ha!* I thought, recognizing it as one of the red lines on my park map. I turned onto the road, which led across a second, much larger stream and along the side of the lake. I paused on a wooden bridge, enjoying the dappled sunlight on the pool underneath it and the playful darting of small fish. I still could not get a clear look at the pond. The stream narrowed as it drew near the shore, and tall briar bushes leaned down to touch its surface. As I leaned on the wooden railing, I heard a faint rumble from the sky. Storm clouds were massing over the surrounding Ramapo Mountains, threatening to cut this particular excursion short.

I still had a few minutes left before the storm arrived, I decided, looking ahead on the dirt road to see whether it was worth continuing my walk. I spotted a few old gravestones underneath a large pine tree and chuckled aloud at the sight. Jeannie would be furious when she realized I had found the old haunted graveyard while she was busy touring the house! Recalling her words about Robert Erskine's grave with the out-of-place bricks and strange lights, I hurried up the path, keeping one eye on the storm clouds in case I needed to turn around quickly.

The first few graves I encountered were from the 1800s; many of the headstones were broken. A few yards farther on, I spotted two rectangular raised tombs made of brick and marble, with small US flags flapping in the ground at each corner. In front of them, near the road, was a boulder with a plaque on it. This had to be General Erskine's grave, I decided, strolling up to the boulder as the hills shivered under another grumble of thunder. I paused to read the plaque and then squinted for a moment at the graves, trying to see a light of some kind or a loose brick. Nothing. *Sorry, Jeannie,* I thought, striding over to the two graves to read the inscriptions. Erskine was buried beside his clerk. There was no sign of Mistress Erskine's grave anywhere.

The storm was approaching rapidly, obliterating the light. A strong breeze sprang up. I was tempted to turn back, but a strange rushing noise like that of continuously falling water had been teasing my ears for quite a while, and I decided to investigate a bit further before turning back. I kept moving along the bank of the pond toward the sound, grinning a bit at the sight of a creepy dead tree with spiderlike bare branches stretching toward the sky. The trunk was half-covered with ivy, the only green on the gray tree. Jeannie would love it. It was the perfect backdrop for a haunted graveyard.

I hurried past the tree and toward the sound of rushing water. The clouds above me were growing thick and dark, and an early twilight was making the woods before and behind me vaguely menacing. I ignored it all, intent on discovery, and a few more yards brought me within sight of a dam with gallons of water hurling across it and down a small waterfall. There came a sudden flash of lightning followed by a huge clap of thunder overhead. I whirled about in surprise, realizing how dark it had become and how far I was from the manor house. The wind was howling through the trees, turning all the leaves upside down, as another bolt of lightning lit up the creepy dead tree by the side of the road. It looked much more menacing in the storm-twilight than when I first saw it.

If I didn't turn back right then, I was liable to get soaked. Unfortunately, retracing my steps meant going under some tall trees, something I didn't relish with all the lightning about. On the other hand, the road ahead also led into the trees and was blocked by a fence. I turned back the way I had come.

Ahead of me, a light suddenly appeared, piercing the gloom of the approaching storm. At first I thought it was the headlights

THE BLUE LANTERN

of a car coming down the dirt road, but as I drew closer, I saw it was a lantern held up by a tall, bearded chap in the costume of a Revolutionary War soldier; he was standing beside the grave of Robert Erskine. An actor, I thought. Jeannie hadn't mentioned any special programs scheduled for today, but perhaps he was one of the regulars. He held the lantern high when he saw me and waited as I raced down the dirt road toward him.

"Cutting it a bit close, eh, laddie?" he asked me in a Scottish burr. "The storm is blowing up quickly." He joined me on the road and we hurried together past the old graveyard, heading toward the bridge. The lantern burned with a blue light that made the man look rather pale and washed out.

"I wanted to get a closer look at the dam," I explained as we crossed the wooden bridge together. "I didn't realize the storm was moving so fast."

"They always do here in the Ramapos," the man said as the lightning and thunder drew closer. The air around us felt thick and heavy. I knew that the heavens would soon open and sheets of rain would soak both of us to the skin. I picked up the pace, practically flying over the dirt and gravel bridge that spanned the smaller stream.

"In my day, I'd turn back to the house at the first sign of a black cloud," the man continued. "Otherwise I was sure to be caught in the rain."

"Who are you supposed to be?" I asked curiously as the large, ornate gates leading to nowhere appeared in front of us.

The man stopped abruptly and I paused, too, turning to face him.

"Where are my manners?" he said ruefully. "Robert Erskine, at your service." He bowed as he introduced himself. The blue lantern flickered in his hand, and a brilliant flash of lightning punctuated his words. I stared at him in shock, realizing that I had seen the flash of lightning *right through his body.*

"You'd best hurry or you'll be caught in the rain," he said to me. "Go on, lad." He gestured toward the house with the blue lantern. Then he vanished into thin air, leaving me alone in the dim twilight of the approaching storm.

I think I screamed, but it was blotted out by another clap of thunder directly over my head. I took to my heels, tearing past the iron gates, up the hill, and down the path in front of the house. I would have fled all the way to the parking lot if Jeannie hadn't called to me from the columned porch. She was standing there with the tour guide, probably discussing ghosts. I didn't wait to find out. I leapt up the steps, caught her around the waist, and said to the man beside her, "So sorry, I just remembered that I left something on the stove." Lifting Jeannie right off her feet, I swept her from the porch, dragged her to the parking lot at a run, and threw her into the car just as the first huge drops of rain started to fall. I flung myself into the driver's seat and started the engine as a sheet of heavy rain thundered against the roof of the vehicle.

"What's the matter?" Jeannie yelled at me over the roar of the rain. "I checked the stove twice before we left!"

I edged the car down the narrow lane leading to the road, barely able to see through the heavy downpour but determined to get away from that haunted place if I had to row the car out.

"Did you meet any ghosts during your tour of the house?" I yelled above the noise of the storm.

"Not one," Jeannie said. "Jim, what is going on?"

"Well *I* met one out by the graveyard," I said, pulling onto

Sloatsburg Road and turning the car toward home. "One Robert Erskine, dressed in a Revolutionary War uniform and carrying a blue lantern. He accompanied me back to the mansion. I thought he was just an actor until I realized that I could *see through his body!*"

Jeannie gaped at me, her mouth hanging open. I eased the car around a bend and up a hill. The downpour made the driving treacherous, but I wanted to get as many miles between me and the surveyor-general's ghost as I reasonably could in such weather conditions.

"You saw his ghost?" Jeannie breathed finally, staring at me in awe.

"I thought you said he appeared as a ball of light over his tombstone. You didn't say anything about a man carrying a lantern," I said accusingly.

"I didn't know," my wife protested. "Did he speak to you? Did you speak to him?"

"We talked about the weather," I said dryly. "He told me to get in out of the rain."

"That's amazing!" Jeannie exclaimed. "You are so lucky!"

"Lucky!" I cried. I was completely freaked out and didn't care if she knew it. "Listen, honey, I thought we had an agreement: You encounter the ghosts and I go hiking."

"You're the one who hiked out to a haunted cemetery," Jeannie reminded me spiritedly. I never could get the best of her in a debate.

I drew in a deep breath, feeling calmer now that we were some distance away from the park. I put on my blinker and pulled out onto the wet highway. The rain was not as heavy here, and I put on a burst of speed.

"Well, I've learned my lesson," I said as I moved into the left lane to avoid a slow car. "The next time you go ghost hunting, I'm going to stay home and read a book."

"Coward," Jeannie jeered.

"You bet!" I said, remembering the way the ghost of Robert Erskine had vanished right before my eyes. The vision of it made me shiver with apprehension and a supernatural fear. "You bet."

2

Public Assist

It was late October, and we were relaxing in the common room of the firehouse, watching TV, when the phone rang at nine o'clock. A call at that time of night usually meant a fire or a public assist of some kind. Only three of us were on duty at the moment: the lieutenant, Dan, and me. I like to be first at things—first to go into a burning house, first to answer the phone, first to the dinner table—so I jogged into the bunk room to the nearest extension to take the call.

"North Plainfield Fire Department," I said into the phone, expecting the dispatcher's voice.

Instead, a woman started babbling to me about an emergency at her house. I couldn't understand what she was saying, except for the words "ghost" and "haunted." I asked her to slow down and tell me what the problem was.

The woman took a deep, calming breath and said, "We need you to come at once. There is a terrible ghost in our house and we want you to remove it."

"A ghost?" I asked incredulously.

The lieutenant's head appeared around the frame of the door. He looked intrigued. "What is it?" he asked. I motioned him to silence and said into the phone, "Lady, this is the fire department. Do you have a fire or an emergency of some kind?"

"Yes, this is an emergency!" the woman said at once. "We have a ghost. Please come!"

She sounded really frightened. I glanced over at the lieutenant, who was bursting with curiosity by this time, and covered the mouthpiece of the phone.

"It's a public assist. Some woman wants us to get rid of a ghost in her house," I told him.

The lieutenant's face lit up with glee. "Oh, we gotta take this call! Dan can hold the fort."

I returned to the phone, got the address of the alleged haunted house, and assured the woman that we would be there as quickly as possible. As I hung up, the lieutenant said that no one had ever called us out for a ghost before.

"Gosh, I wonder why?" I replied dryly, checking my bunker pants to make sure I had everything I needed before we drove away in one of the fire engines.

"We probably don't need to turn on the emergency lights," the lieutenant said, rather reluctantly.

"For a ghost?" I asked. "Not unless you think they'll scare it away!"

The lieutenant chuckled as we made our way to the house, which was less than five minutes from the station. I turned the fire engine onto a dark, gloomy street and pulled up in front of a huge two-family house. The place was dilapidated and old, with a sagging porch and roof, peeling paint, and cracked windows. Several shaggy trees loomed over it, and the grass in the yard was overgrown. In short, it looked like a haunted house, except for several cars that lined the driveway. There were only a few flickering lights shining through dirty windows.

Two women and two children were huddled in the center of the lawn. It was a windy, chilly night—not a night to linger outside. *These people must really be afraid,* I thought. The lieutenant and I hurried over to them.

"Did you call about a ghost?" I asked.

"Yes!" a short, plump woman with dark hair said excitedly. "That was me. There is a ghost inside our house!"

"How do you know it's a ghost?" asked the lieutenant.

"We were sitting in the living room after dinner when it started groaning," the second woman—introduced as a sister—said, waving her arms expressively. "The walls shook with the sound. Moaning and shrieking and hissing!"

The children, a little boy and girl, gasped and clung to their mother, staring wide-eyed at their aunt and nodding in agreement.

"I came out here at once with the children while Mary called for help," the sister finished.

"We'll take a look around," said the lieutenant. "Why don't you come back into the house where it's warm?"

They said no most emphatically. The children started trembling and crying at the very notion, and the women were ready to pack up and leave at once if we found anything.

"I am sure everything will be fine," the lieutenant said soothingly. I suggested that the family get into the car where they could stay warm. They agreed to do so, and the women begged us to be careful.

We climbed onto the sagging porch. I was first, as always, and I approached the front door with interest, wondering what I would find.

The storm door was rattling all by itself.

I stopped abruptly, and the lieutenant knocked into me. "What is it?" he asked. I pointed at the door. Now he could hear it, too. *Rattle, buzz, rattle, rattle.* The door was shaking. I felt goose bumps rise on my arms, and for the first time I wondered if there really might be a ghost of some kind in this spooky old house.

"Wow. Creepy," said the lieutenant. He didn't sound nearly as cocky as he had out on the lawn, but his words drove away my unspoken dread. This was a public assist, so we needed to assist. There is, I assured myself as I opened the quivering storm door, no such thing as a ghost. I grasped the handle of the front door and turned it.

Ooooooooooooo. We were greeted with a long, low moan.

"Good Lord, what is that?" asked the lieutenant as I edged into the dark hallway.

A staircase led up to the rooms where a second family lived, but they were away for the night. Our family lived on the ground floor, so I turned to the right and entered the door to their apartment. As we made our way into the dimly lit front room, the walls rattled and an occasional thump made my heart leap into my throat.

Ooooooooooooo. The walls moaned, followed by *rattle, rattle, thump, swish.* My goose bumps returned, but I could see nothing suspicious or out of the ordinary around me. The lieutenant and I decided to check the utilities in the basement, a common procedure in public assist cases. He was right on my heels as we made our way through the living room and into the kitchen, where the basement door was rattling and shaking as badly as the storm door outside.

Oooooooooooo, the house groaned. *Ahhhhhhhhhhhh.*

Gingerly, as if I were about to touch something hot, I turned the handle. The door opened with a little whoosh of air, and all the sounds stopped.

"I think you just let the ghost out," the lieutenant joked feebly.

There was dead silence throughout the house.

"Well, we'd still better check things out down here," I said uneasily. I was more disconcerted by the sudden silence than I had been by the groaning.

I turned on the light. A dusty, bare bulb lit up the staircase but did nothing to illuminate the rest of the huge basement. As I started down the long, rickety wooden staircase, I expected a skeletal hand to reach through the openings between the treads and grab my ankles. Behind me I could hear the lieutenant breathing more quickly than normal, and I wondered if he was seeing the same monstrous shadows that were making my heart pound. When my feet touched the basement floor, the sounds started all over again.

Oooooooooooo. Rattle, rattle, thump, swish. Only it was much louder down here, and a new sound joined the others.

Hissssssss went the walls.

Oooooooooooo groaned the floorboards above us.

Thump! Thump! Rattle, rattle, rattle.

I scoped out the place and realized that the furnace, water heater, and other utilities were—of course—on the far side of the dim junk- and cobweb-filled basement. I reached into the pocket of my bunker pants for the flashlight I always carried and was horrified to discover it wasn't there.

PUBLIC ASSIST

Oooooooooooo. Ahhhhhhhhhhhhh.

"'Ooh, aah is right!" I muttered back as I edged through the clutter. There were pillars throughout the basement, supporting dusty brick archways. Cobwebs hung so low that they brushed my hair and face. The light from the single bulb by the staircase threw strange shadows over mildewed piles of clothes, broken furniture, half-assembled bicycles, and ancient steamer trunks.

Hisssssss. Oooooooooooo. Thump! Thump! Rattle, rattle. Hissssssss.

I spotted another lightbulb about halfway down the long cellar. The chain was only two inches long; when I leapt up to pull it, cobwebs covered my face, clinging to my eyes and mouth. The bulb feebly flickered to life as the walls continued to hiss softly.

I hurried over to the utilities: two furnaces and a water heater. I went to the old furnace first and started going through the normal procedures—turning it off, checking various parts. The lieutenant was doing the same thing for the water heater. As we both moved to the new furnace, we realized that the ominous noises were fading away. We paused in our work and stared at each other across the murky air.

"No way," said the lieutenant. "No way was all that noise caused by the furnace!"

With a last, sad *Ooooooooo,* the sounds faded into silence.

I nodded. "It was the furnace."

Just to make sure, I turned the old furnace back on. Within moments, the walls were hissing, groaning, and rattling at us with renewed energy and enthusiasm. I turned it back off. The sounds slowly faded away.

The lieutenant started laughing, and I joined him.

"For a few minutes," he said, "I thought that I was going to have to start believing in ghosts!"

"Me, too," I said, smiling in relief. We decided that the hissing sound was made by the hot water flowing through the pipes. The moans, groans, rattles, and thumps were caused by loose pipes that had lost their seals over the years and were vibrating and moving inside the walls.

But there was one mystery left to solve: "Why were the doors shaking?" the lieutenant asked.

"Look at this place," I said, gesturing to the small, sealed windows at the top of the walls. "It's tightly sealed. The furnace couldn't get enough air and was trying to draw it from upstairs and from outside. That's what made the doors rattle. The sounds stopped for a few minutes when we opened the basement door because some of the air the furnace needed rushed in."

We finished the routine checks, turned the furnace back on, and went through the moaning house and outside to talk to the family. They flatly refused to believe us when we said it was the furnace that had caused the noises, not a ghost. The lieutenant finally persuaded them to come into the groaning, rattling house. We took Mary—the mother of the two children—down to the basement and turned the furnace off and on for her several times to prove that it was the source of the ghostly noises. She finally believed us, but as we left the house, we could hear her trying in vain to convince her sister and the children that their house was not haunted.

As we climbed into the fire engine, the lieutenant seemed puzzled. "I don't know how I am going to write this one up for the books," he said.

"Better you than me!" I said as I drove us back to the station.

3

In the Fog

It was one of those gray, foggy mornings that never seem to turn into true day. I hate those mornings. The fog was everywhere, creating a swirling, misty effect that made it difficult to see as I drove to the train station. Not good. I'd already had a cup of coffee, but I still felt half asleep.

I groped my way blindly onto the commuter train to Jersey City, a second cup of coffee clutched in my hand. I fell into a seat with a sigh and almost immediately dozed off as the train started the regular *rattle, shake, bump, hum* it always made when it headed down the tracks. I opened my eyes briefly to show my commuter ID to the cheerful, round-faced conductor. Then I spread my things out onto the seat next to me, which had remained empty, and tried to catch a few extra winks.

What brought me back to consciousness was extreme cold. At first I thought that someone had opened a window, but when I looked around, all the windows were closed. The fog outside was thicker than ever, making it difficult to see more than a foot or so out the windows. I shivered and buttoned my suit jacket, but I still felt a terrible chill in my bones.

For a moment the world around me seemed to flicker in response to the cold. The train slowed and began making the *choom-choom, chugga-chugga-chugga* sounds I associated with old-time steam trains. Outside the fog thinned; suddenly I could see trees and buildings and people again. I gasped in shock and leaned toward the window glass, the cold forgotten, as a horse and buggy flashed by on a dirt road near the tracks. I rubbed my eyes. There had never been a dirt road there before! I had been riding this line for six months, and I had not once seen any of the people or buildings now visible though the light fog that still swirled everywhere.

There were businessmen wearing fancy waistcoats and jackets in a style popular in the 1880s. There were women wearing long skirts and fancy shirts or very beautiful long dresses, strolling in small groups and entering shops. There were farmers with horse-drawn wagons, and a line of children being hustled toward a building that was obviously a schoolhouse. They were accompanied by a pretty woman who seemed to be their teacher. A telegraph pole passed the window as we moved away from the strange town and out into open fields.

I must be dreaming, I thought, turning away from the window. It was a very vivid, very cold dream. I shivered and looked back inside the commuter train, then gasped again when I realized that it had changed, too. The bright electric lights, slightly dingy walls, and well-worn seats of the train I took every day had been replaced by fancy dark paneling, plush seats, and brass fixtures. Gas lights flickered faintly. It was a scene from more than a hundred years ago. An old-time conductor wearing a round hat with a stiff brim came down the aisle, taking tickets

IN THE FOG

from my fellow passengers, all of whom were men in 1880s business clothes; many sported mustaches and beards.

Trembling violently, I pinched myself, trying to wake up from this very real dream—but somehow I knew I was already awake. The conductor's face was gray over his crisp uniform; his cheeks were hollow, and his eyes had sunk deep into their sockets. He looked like a walking corpse, though none of the gentlemen riding the train seemed to notice anything amiss.

The temperature dropped another ten degrees as the conductor approached my seat. I handed him my commuter pass with shaking hands, wondering what he would make of it. But as soon as he took it, it transformed into the same kind of ticket everyone around me had given him.

"It was a foggy day like this one when it happened," the conductor said to me as he handed back the pass. He had a deep, sepulchral voice that sent shivers racing down my spine.

"When what happened?" I asked, trying to keep my teeth from chattering as I spoke.

"The train wreck," intoned the conductor. "It was a day much like today. The engineer was driving a long freight train with a big six-driver engine. He was pulling a lot of empties except for the last three or four cars, which were carrying some very heavy freight. The freight train was scheduled right behind a passenger train, and the engineer was trailing her real close when he entered a thick patch of fog. Suddenly, he could not see the passenger train in front of him or anything to the sides."

The conductor paused, staring out the window. He gestured toward the fog-filled fields.

"It happened yonder, where the fog is so dense. Afraid he might hit the passenger train ahead of him, the engineer panicked and slammed the steam brakes as hard as he could. Sparks flew from the tires of the drivers as the fifty-five-ton engine came to a sudden halt. The heavy cars at the end of the train kept moving forward, pushing hard into the empty cars just behind the engine. The cars in the middle buckled under the opposing forces; they were pushed straight up off the tracks until they were as high as a nearby telegraph pole. For a moment, the train resembled a drawn bow. Then the cars snapped; one flew right over the telegraph wire and landed in that field, while the others fell over with a mighty crash."

I listened in horror to the story.

"Was anyone hurt?" I asked.

"There was a conductor braking in the middle of the train," the hollow-faced man said. "He lived in the house next to the depot we just passed. He was squeezed to death, and his body landed in the field with the freight car."

The conductor looked me straight in the eye. "They say that the conductor is doomed to walk the trains on this route, telling the story of the wreck, until someone believes his tale of a freight car that flipped over the top of a twenty-foot-high telegraph wire."

I sat bolt upright, shaking like a leaf and unable to take my eyes away from his.

"Would you believe his tale?" the cadaverous conductor asked me.

I shivered, terrified by the red gleam I could see flickering at the back of his dark eyes.

"Yes, I would," I said.

The whole world went white for a moment, and I thought I heard a laugh of triumph somewhere at the edges of time. Then

I was staring into the round face of the chubby conductor who had looked at my commuter pass when I first entered the train. Electric lights brightened the familiar dingy interior, and thick fog obscured the view outside.

"I said, 'Are you all right?'" the chubby conductor repeated, tapping me on the shoulder. "You look like you've seen a ghost."

I took a deep breath. "I'm fine. Thanks."

The conductor nodded, still eyeing me with concern. He moved on slowly, and I slumped back into the seat and took a sip of coffee with shaking hands. I was still trembling as we drew into the station, and my legs barely held me when I got out of the train. I looked around me suspiciously, but everyone and everything looked reassuringly modern. Still, I didn't feel safe until I was in my office with the door closed behind me. I kept seeing the pale man in the crisp uniform, his eyes flickering red as he told his story, and hearing his laugh of triumph when I told him I believed it. I wasn't sure if I had really seen a ghost or just had a terrible dream.

To my relief, the fog had cleared by the time I left work that evening, and my trip home was uneventful. Later, I did some research on that particular branch of the railroad, to see if anyone had ever reported an accident like the one the ghost-conductor had recounted. I learned that a train had derailed one foggy morning in the 1880s in the area that had been pointed out to me by the ghost. And the only casualty had been the conductor braking in the middle of the train!

4

The Mark of the Spirit Hand

ANDOVER

Well now, Bailey, Hill, and Evans were three of the most rascally chaps that had ever lived in Andover, make no mistake! They were a trio of hooligans as children. They had lived on neighboring farms growing up and had wreaked more havoc than any three boys before or since. They all married around the same time and were good husbands and fathers. But they were the absolute despair of their God-fearing wives since Bailey was an atheist, Hill was an agnostic, and Evans called himself a skeptic. Never to church would any of them go, though their wives begged and pleaded with them. Evans was considered the most "religious" by the trio; he had been to church once to see his eldest son baptized. All three men were retired and alone now, except for each other. Their wives had passed on, and their descendants were scattered all over the United States.

Pals to the end, Bailey, Hill, and Evans had sold off their farms and rented a nice old cottage just outside Andover, not too far from the place where they had grown up. Those rascals spent their days smoking and fishing and drinking and playing cards and chasing all the local widows. The churchgoing folks in town shook their heads whenever they spoke of the merry old

bachelors who, if they weren't runnir
ruckus, were in the tavern discussing
horse racing, and religion.

The minister of the local church
them once, but he came away from
head and muttering words like "!
Bailey, Hill, and Evans treated the whole matter
relived the scene for more than a month over cards at the tavern.

One evening, as they were sitting around their favorite table near the bar, the conversation turned to the afterlife. The old bachelors discussed the various beliefs held by religions across the world, arguing the pros and cons of each with skeptical enthusiasm. As they finished their last round of the evening, Evans made a merry proposition: Whoever died first would come back from the grave—if he could—and reveal himself to the other two, thus confirming that there was an afterlife. Hill and Bailey were much taken with his proposal. Hill laid his four-fingered right hand (his index finger had been cut off by an axe in childhood) over his heart and vowed solemnly to return should he be the unlucky first. Bailey and Evans cheered heartily and echoed his vow, and the three old bachelors drank to their shared pledge.

Perhaps it was only coincidence. Perhaps it was fate. Whatever the reason, Hill died in his sleep that very night. Evans and Bailey were shaken by his death. There followed a period of weeks in which the remaining bachelors were not seen at the tavern. However, life soon settled into a new routine, and the two men returned to their favorite table. Each night, they drank a toast to their dearly departed friend, who had not returned from the grave, thus confirming Bailey's atheism and Evans's skepticism.

after Hill's death, Evans and Bailey left the tavern later than usual, having spent the evening playing cards with a couple of friends who had come to visit from out of town. They walked home under a moonless sky, singing a rather naughty song and talking off and on about Hill. After several false starts, they managed to drag each other through the front door of the cottage and eventually found the staircase leading up to their rooms on the second floor.

Evans called "good night" to his old pal and staggered into his room. He pulled off his boots and yanked on his nightshirt. Then he removed his nightshirt, took off his clothes, and put the nightshirt back on. "Silly, drunken old fool," he scolded himself with a chuckle.

Evans clapped his nightcap onto his head, groped his way under the covers of the bed, and blew out the candle. He was almost asleep when a bright light pierced his eyelids.

"Cut it out, Bailey," Evans muttered, turning over and hiding his head under the pillow. The light grew brighter, and a chill wind swept through the room, pulling the covers off the bed. Annoyed, Evans rolled over and sat up, ready to scold his old pal for playing jokes on him. But the words died on the tip of his tongue.

Standing next to his bed was the shining figure of Hill. He looked much the same as he had in life, except there was a youthfulness about him and a new sense of wholeness, as if he had found the true secret of life and happiness. Evans was both terrified and awed by the sight of his friend. Hill reached out his four-fingered hand and laid it on Evans's shoulder. The ghost's touch was like a cold fire that burned his skin. For a long moment the two men gazed into each other's eyes. Then Hill disappeared.

Evans gave a cry of shock and distress. His shoulder throbbed where Hill had touched him, and he clutched it, hunching over in pain, his whole body trembling with the shock of the encounter. Bailey must have heard his cry, because he came into the darkened room with a hastily lit lantern.

"Evans, what's wrong?" Bailey exclaimed, staring at his friend.

"He was here," Evans gasped.

"Who was here?" Bailey asked, setting his lantern on the table and coming to stand beside Evans.

"Hill was here," Evans said, shaking violently at the memory. "He stood where you are now and touched me on the shoulder!"

Evans pulled back the collar of his nightshirt, and both men stared at his bare shoulder. A white, four-fingered impression of a hand was burned into Evans's skin where the ghost had touched him. The scar was completely healed over, as if Evans had received the burn many weeks ago rather than just a moment before. Bailey gasped and stepped backward, sinking into a wooden chair next to the bedstand. Evans gingerly poked at the mark on his shoulder, flinching a bit although it didn't hurt.

"It was Hill," he repeated, staring at Bailey in the flickering lantern light. "It was Hill."

The mark of the four-fingered hand remained permanently branded on Evans's shoulder. He and Bailey stopped going to the tavern after that fateful night. The minister of the local church almost had a heart attack the next Sunday when the old bachelors slipped into the pew at the front of the sanctuary and sheepishly tried to hide behind a hymnal. The two men were

THE MARK OF THE SPIRIT HAND

greeted with open arms by all the good folk of the congregation, and the minister shook their hands heartily after the service. Evans and Bailey never told anyone what prompted their sudden conversion, and folks gave up asking after a few months.

Sometimes during the weekly sermons, Evans could be seen rubbing his shoulder thoughtfully, as if he were trying to ease a sore muscle. And whenever the minister spoke of the afterlife in his sermons, Bailey would glance over at his friend significantly and say a hearty "Amen."

5

The Searcher

LONG BEACH ISLAND

Have you seen my love? I have searched for him everywhere, but I cannot find him. Can you tell me where he is?

I ask these questions of everyone I see, reaching out to touch their shoulders or their arms. My hand goes right through them as if they were made of mist. Most people act as if they cannot see me at all, merely shuddering as if they were cold and walking quickly away. Sometimes people scream when they see me, as if they are looking at a ghost, and then run in the opposite direction. They never answer my questions.

The beach seems endless as I walk from one end of the island to the other, down the long, long miles and back again. He must be here. I know he is here. He would never desert me. Perhaps he is injured! Perhaps he is ill. My fear presses me ever onward. I stop each person I meet to ask the same question over and over: Have you seen my love?

There were only the three of us in my family growing up— Mama, Papa, and me. Papa was a fisherman, a surprisingly prosperous one. He was a tall, red-haired man with a bushy brown beard who often brought home jewelry and trinkets for my fair-haired little Mama and for me. I remember dressing up in front of Mama's mirror, draping myself in ropes of pearls, winding flowers into my blond curls, and putting on every ring and pin Papa had ever given her. I told Mama I was a princess, and she laughed and ruffled my hair.

Mama and I were active in our local church, though Papa rarely attended. It was from the women at church that I first heard about the wreckers. The Ladies' Sewing Circle came to our house one week, and we all sat around our parlor doing hand-sewing and talking over the latest news. According to the ladies, the wreckers knew that many of the ships traveling to and from New York tried to stay as close to shore as possible to cut time and distance off their journey. They sailed by landmarks during the day and navigated by the stars at night, avoiding the shoals and other hazards as best they could.

Ships often tried to "cut the corner" around Long Beach Island, and the wreckers took advantage of this practice. On dark and moonless nights, they would lead their mules or horses or cows up and down the beach after dark with bright lanterns strapped to their harnesses. They were trying to fool the helmsmen of passing ships into believing that the lights they saw came from another ship sailing close to the shore. The helmsmen would steer in closer to the other "ship," and their vessels would smash into the shoals. The dead sailors would float ashore to be robbed of their possessions by the wreckers.

When Mama caught a glimpse of my terrified fascination with these tales, she hushed the ladies and changed the topic to something more suitable for a child's ears. Her best friend immediately produced an entertaining anecdote about some local pigs and a rambunctious little boy that made the whole Sewing Circle laugh until they cried.

That was the last time I heard Mama laugh. She fell ill with a terrible fever soon afterward. Though her life was spared, she would never again take more than a few steps from her bed. I was ten the year Mama lost her health—old enough to help out around the house and take care of Mama. Only there was one task I was not prepared for.

One night Papa awakened me from my sleep and bade me follow him down to the beach. I was horrified when I saw a ship sinking off the shore. I thought we were there to rescue the sailors, but Papa told me gruffly that there was nothing we could do for them. As we reached the beach, I saw men's bodies washing ashore. It was a shocking moment. I had never seen a corpse before, and the poor mangled bodies of the drowned sailors turned my stomach. I ran quickly into the bushes and was sick.

Papa shouted at me then, telling me to stop acting like a woman and get to work. "Doing what?" I asked him. We were there, he explained, to remove money and jewelry and anything of value from the sailors, seeing that they did not need it any more. I protested strongly. Such a thing was wrong, I told him. Only the most unscrupulous people looted the bodies of shipwreck victims. The folks in town despised looters almost as much as they did wreckers.

Papa struck me across the face then and told me to obey him or find somewhere else to live. With trembling hands, I did as he asked, knowing it was wrong, but not knowing what else to do. Where could I go? All my parents' relatives were dead. And even if there was somewhere to go, how could I leave my invalid mother? So I knelt beside each poor sailor, praying softly for his soul as I took away his worldly goods.

Several more times that year, Papa dragged me down to the beach to loot the bodies along with the shadow figures of many other men and women. I never looked at any of them closely, not wanting to recognize someone I knew. Whenever I resisted, Papa beat me. I was ashamed when I realized that this, not fishing, was the source of his prosperity. I never told Mama how Papa came by his additional income, as the knowledge would have killed her.

I found out by accident that Papa himself was one of the wreckers, not just someone who profited from them. One moonless night, after I tucked Mama into her bed, I heard a man come to the window to talk with Papa. They spoke of borrowing a few mules, which didn't make much sense to me at the time. Later, when Papa dragged me down to a shipwreck, I understood. The borrowed mules had been used to carry deceptive lights up and down the beach, luring the poor ship to its doom.

As soon as we returned home, I ran into my room and sank onto my bed, muffling my sobs with a pillow. How could Papa do such a thing? It was murder, plain and simple. And how could I live with myself—I, who went down to the beaches with him to steal from the dead? My tears ceased at last and were replaced by a numbness that stole over my mind and soul.

That was the last time I ever thought or cried over my situation. In the years that followed, I let the numbness fill me, and I no longer prayed over the dead sailors when I stripped them of their worldly goods. I just followed Papa when he bade me come to the beach with him. The rest of the time I took care of Mama, cleaned the little gray house where we lived, went to school and to church on Sunday (though I was too ashamed to pray for redemption from my secret crimes), and attended the local Sewing Circle.

When I was eighteen, a handsome young sailor named Kenny took notice of me and started walking me home from socials and from church. He was dark-haired and blue-eyed with a dimple in his chin and a small white scar on his right cheek. I thought him wise and witty and completely wonderful. For the first time since I turned ten, the numbness around my heart lifted, and I dared to fall in love. Perhaps (oh please, God!) we would marry. Perhaps I could leave this terrible house and take Mama away with me. Perhaps there would be redemption at last from my crimes against the dead.

I never told Kenny about Papa and the wreckers, but just being with him gave me the strength to defy Papa. I refused to help him loot the bodies of the poor sailors the next time a ship wrecked near our beach. Papa was furious with me. He hit me so hard that I lost consciousness, and he had to go to the beaches alone. The next morning I made up a story to explain my blackened eye and bruised face to Mama. I stayed away from town until the bruises healed, not wanting Kenny to see me that way, not knowing how to explain. I was afraid he would turn from me in disgust when he realized what a terrible creature I was.

Kenny proposed marriage after courting me for two months. I was never so happy in my life as the moment I agreed to be his wife! He set sail for the West Indies the next day, promising that when he returned we would be married and live on the other side of the island. He didn't understand why I insisted that Mama come with us; surely Papa would want to care for his own wife, Kenny said. But I told him that Papa did not have time and that Mama would be better off in our new home.

Kenny's voyage took several months; the time he was away seemed like an eternity. I was not sure I would be able to defy Papa without Kenny around to offer unwitting support. Fortunately, there was a long spell with no shipwrecks, and I was spared the choice.

Then Mama fell ill again. She grew weaker and weaker, and I spent most of my time nursing her, terrified that she would die and leave me alone with Papa. I prayed and prayed that Kenny would come home soon and take us away with him.

I had just gotten Mama to sleep late one evening when Papa came hurrying into our little gray house. There was a shipwreck on the shore nearby, and we were going to loot it. My face flushed as I told him I would not go. Papa slapped me, and I fell heavily against the sharp edge of the table, which pierced my side. I felt several ribs snap inside me and imagined their shattered remnants slicing my torso apart. The pain was devastating. I sank to the floor and curled into a ball of agony.

Papa grabbed me by my long hair and lifted me up to face him. I heard him threaten to go into the bedroom and tell Mama about his wrecking. He knew, as I did, that the secret would kill her. I thought of Kenny. If I went with Papa, I would lose Kenny, for an upright man would never bind himself to someone involved in an act as evil as wrecking. But if I didn't go, I would kill my mother. There was but one option.

Anger and guilt overwhelmed me as I dragged myself down to the beach behind Papa. The physical pain was intense, radiating out from my ribs and inner organs through my chest and stomach. I could barely walk and had to stop several times to retch and spit up blood. Somewhere in the back of my head, I knew that I was dying; you couldn't cough up so much blood and live. But my physical agony was nothing compared to my emotional despair as I saw my last hope of redemption fading away.

I stumbled onto the beach, nearly bent double as I clutched my injured side. As I stared at the familiar scene of carnage that followed a wreck, I felt the numbness stealing back into my heart and mind, and I knew then that I was lost.

A body was lying face down only a few steps from me, though I almost missed it due to a growing darkness around the edges of my vision. Nonetheless, I had to make an effort or Papa would keep his promise to tell Mama the awful truth. I dropped my lantern beside the body and knelt. Through glazed eyes, I searched the dead man's pockets for money or jewelry. There was nothing. Then I turned him over.

It was a young fellow, dark-haired and blue-eyed with a dimple in his chin. For a moment my vision cleared, and I stared into the sailor's face, his features etching themselves into my brain for all eternity. I felt something in my mind give way, and everything around me went blurry and still and calm. When I focused once more on the handsome face of the drowned sailor, I felt pity for him but had no recollection of who he was or how he came to be on the beach. Then pain from my broken ribs swelled up inside me, driving out the numbness in one final burst. I saw a terrible pit open before my eyes, and I could do nothing to save myself from falling down and down and down into its bottomless depths. I coughed, my body wracked with suffering. Blood spilled over my dress, over the sailor's clothes, over his beloved, dead face. I collapsed slowly on top of him, feeling my life fading away into pain and darkness and death.

And then I was standing on a strange beach, looking down on a scene that I was sure had some significance to me, if I could

THE SEARCHER

only remember what it was. A young girl with flowing blond hair lay sprawled across the body of a handsome sailor. They were both covered with blood, their faces lit eerily by a lantern resting beside them.

I wanted to help them, but there was nothing I could do. And I couldn't linger, because deep inside my soul I felt a sharp compulsion that could not be denied. My love, my heart, my soul, my redemption was missing. Kenny was out there somewhere, if I could only find him. I had to find him, or all was lost!

I turned away from the poor dead couple and saw a tall, red-haired man with a bushy brown beard standing a few feet away. He was holding a darkened lantern and was staring at the dead couple with horror on his face. I wondered if the man was somehow acquainted with one of them.

I did not want to interrupt such a personal moment, but desperation drove me over to his side. I had to find Kenny, and maybe this man could help. I reached out to tap the man's shoulder, but my hand went right through him as if he were made of mist. He shuddered when I touched him. I stared pleadingly into his face, compelling him to see me, to speak to me, but he was blind to all but the dead couple lying on the ground in front of him. Still, I asked him the questions burning through my mind, though he gave me no response.

"Have you seen my love? I have searched for him everywhere, but I cannot find him. Can you tell me where he is?"

6

The Author Returns

She fell in love with the house as soon as she saw it. Perched on top of a hill overlooking Pompton Lake, the huge Victorian had a wraparound porch, high ceilings, a beautiful octagonal dining room, and a fireplace right beside the grand staircase in the entryway. The staircase resembled the letter *J*. The longest section descended steeply from the second floor, stopping abruptly three-quarters of the way down at a small landing; the staircase then turned to complete the short section of the *J* with three stairs leading to the floor beside the fireplace.

There was a square window with inset stained glass in the wall above the landing, but the wall behind the main section of the staircase was rather bare. She decided at once that it needed something—a large portrait perhaps, or some framed picture that would take up several yards of blank wall.

The house, like all Victorians, tended to ramble here and there. The upper hallway twisted and turned, and there was a servants' staircase that led from the ground-floor kitchen all the way up to the attic, where the servants had probably slept at one time.

What she liked most about the house was its connection to a local author. The sister of Albert Payson Terhune, an early twentieth-century collie breeder who wrote *Lad, a Dog* and many other books, had lived there. Terhune's famous home, Sunnybank, which was featured in many of his books, was on the western shore of Pompton Lake, almost directly opposite. The author had often swum across the lake to visit his sister.

Due to its advanced age, the Victorian was not the easiest house to maintain. It made a lot of rattles and creaks and funny sounds—but none of these things mattered to the prospective owner, who bought it and moved in immediately.

She was a bit surprised by the cautious attitude of her new neighbors when they spoke to her. She didn't understand what was inhibiting them until someone let it slip that the neighbors all believed that the Victorian house was haunted. The new owner was delighted at the thought, although she did not believe in ghosts herself. A house such as this deserved a ghostly reputation, and thereafter she shivered deliciously whenever it creaked and rattled.

The new owner asked around and soon learned a few of the tales associated with the house. Footsteps were sometimes heard in the upper hallway when only one person was home. The invisible walker would hurry down the servants' staircase, through the kitchen, and out the back door. And a guest had once heard someone walking outside the door of his room and called out, thinking that his wife was approaching. The woman's voice that answered was that of a complete stranger. When he got up to see who it was, there was no one in the hallway.

The new owner had yet to hear any of these mysterious sounds herself, although her son claimed that one afternoon shortly after they moved in, he had heard the inner door to the foyer rattling all by itself, followed by the sound of footsteps

THE AUTHOR RETURNS

mounting the main staircase and walking down the second-floor hallway.

Undaunted, the new owner threw herself into decorating the house, adding personal touches to the spacious rooms. Over several weeks, it began to feel like home. But she still had not found a picture to hang in the stairwell.

Then, one day she heard that Sunnybank was going to be torn down. She was shocked by the news and saddened that the town would soon be deprived of such a historic house, the one where Albert Payson Terhune had lived and written and raised his famous collie dogs. All of the Sunnybank furnishings were going to be auctioned off, and she felt it appropriate to bid on some of them and put them into the house where Terhune's sister once resided.

At the auction, the first thing the new owner saw was an eight-foot reproduction of a Dutch painting called *Christ before the High Priest*. It would be perfect for the wall behind the staircase. She bid on it, won it, and had it brought to her home across the lake for installation. It looked absolutely stunning on the wall in the stairwell, and she frequently paused to admire it from the foyer.

The new owner was studying the painting one afternoon when her eye was caught by the figure of a man hurrying down the main staircase from the second floor. This stranger was very tall, with ruggedly handsome features and broad shoulders. She was startled by the unexpectedness of his appearance.

"Who are you?" she demanded at once. "What are you doing in my house?"

The man stopped on the small landing and looked at her over the banister. The large picture from the Terhune estate framed the back of his head. That was when she recognized her visitor: It was Terhune himself, the original owner of the painting. She was seeing a ghost!

She shivered, her arms breaking out in goose bumps as she and Terhune stared at one another for a timeless moment. Then the ghost disappeared. She sank down onto the closest chair, shaking from head to toe. Her son entered the room a moment later and came over to her quickly when he saw her agitation.

"What is it? What's wrong?" he asked. She told him what she had seen.

"So, it's Terhune who has been haunting this house," her son mused, looking up at the stairwell.

She shook her head. "I think that Terhune's ghost came here with the painting," she said. "The other footsteps sounded on the servants' staircase, and the voice that was heard belonged to a woman."

"But I heard someone come in the front door and walk up the grand staircase," her son said. "And that is where you saw Terhune."

She nodded thoughtfully. "Perhaps we have two ghosts," she concluded.

Her son grinned. "Still want to live in the house?" he asked teasingly.

She considered his question for a moment, remembering the look she had shared with the author. Then she smiled.

"Yes, I do," she said.

And so they remained in the house where Terhune's sister had once lived. Although the new owner heard occasional footsteps on the staircases or the second floor, she never saw the ghost of Albert Payson Terhune again.

7

The Figure in the Window

PEAPACK

The three of us were hanging around the local diner, drinking coffee late one evening, when Alec said he wanted to go up to Peapack to check out a house for sale. I had volunteered to drive that night since Alec, my boyfriend, drives like a maniac and I value my skin too highly to get into a car with him behind the wheel. I thought it was a funny time of night to be checking out houses, but both Alec and his pal Steve were eloquently enthusiastic about the idea, so I agreed to the trip.

Once in the car, we turned up the radio and shouted back and forth over the blaring music. I asked Alec what was so special about this particular house, and he said it was an old, rundown Italianate mansion with twenty-six fireplaces, an indoor swimming pool, and a squash court. It used to be owned by nuns but had been abandoned. Furthermore, it sat on fifty acres of property, including beautifully terraced grounds and a pond. The grounds were being used temporarily by some hunting club, Alec added, and the members sometimes rode their horses around at night, armed with rifles. I gave him a sideways glance, thinking he was kidding. Apparently, he wasn't.

I fell silent while the guys started singing off-key to the music on the radio. I was feeling nervous about the whole thing—hunters with rifles, a derelict mansion that was supposedly for sale, and a boyfriend who wanted to visit the house at 11:00 p.m. without a Realtor. I was convinced that Alec was more interested in adventure than in real estate! However, in for a penny, in for a pound, as the saying goes. We were almost there, and what was the worst that could happen? Surely the horsemen wouldn't shoot anyone they found on the grounds . . . or would they?

We pulled off the road and parked the car near a wooded area, at the back of the property. The mansion itself was at the top of a hill, still quite a distance away. I glanced around for No Trespassing signs but didn't see any. Of course, it was a cloudy, dark night and the roadside was pitch black with no streetlamps. Still, I reasoned that if I didn't see any signs, then I could claim ignorance should any night-riding horseman take offense at my presence on the grounds! Shivering half with fear and half with excitement, I followed Alec and Steve into the woods.

It was a fairly long and spooky walk, with only one flashlight to guide us. I kept shying at shadows, expecting a galloping figure to accost us at any second. But we saw no one and heard only the nocturnal noises one would expect in the woods.

We came out onto an overgrown lawn looking up toward several terraces that stretched up and up and up, finally ending at the back of the mansion. The house was, Alec informed us, a fine example of Italianate architecture. Alec is cute, but he can be irritatingly pompous at times.

I nervously followed Alec and Steve up the stairs to the first- and then the second-tier terrace. The mansion loomed tall and ominous in the darkness, and the flashlight did little to illuminate our surroundings. The wind shook the treetops and moaned through the overgrown shrubbery. I kept expecting crazy men on horseback or scary axe-murderers to reach out and grab me as I dogged the heels of my boyfriend and his pal. This would be a perfect spot for a Halloween party, I decided.

When we reached the top terrace, Alec and Steve moved toward the back doors of the mansion, determined to find a way inside. I hung back. There was no way I was going any closer to that creepy monstrosity, with its many dark windows and derelict air. I stood listening to the guys murmuring to each other as they tried the nearest door. Then I glanced up at the third story. The dormered windows gaped like dark eyes staring out over the bleak, abandoned grounds. I trembled. Talk about atmosphere! All this house needed was a stringed orchestra playing eerie music to complete the scene.

Suddenly, a ball of light appeared in the third-story window on the far right. I blinked in surprise, because I was sure Alec had said the house was abandoned. The light seemed to float, as if it were a globe of some sort rather than an overhead fixture. Before my astonished gaze, it expanded and formed into a glowing human figure. A ghostly white light gleamed all around the body, and the slight figure radiated with an unearthly fire. I could not make out any features, but I got a very strong sense of femininity. I gasped in shock, my heart pounding so hard in my chest that I thought it would explode.

I tore my gaze away from the window, calling out to Alec. When I looked up again, the figure was gone.

"Alec," I whispered urgently. "Let's get out of here!"

THE FIGURE IN THE WINDOW

Something in my tone penetrated my boyfriend's admittedly thick head, and he and Steve loped over to where I was standing. As soon as they reached me, I turned and started hurrying down the steps of the upper terrace. Within three steps I began running, and when we reached level ground, I took off at a pace that the best Olympic athlete would have had trouble matching. Behind me, I could hear Alec and Steve shouting back and forth to each other. They were saying something about keys, but I didn't stop to find out more. I just wanted to put as much distance as possible between myself and that . . . that glowing thing.

I had the engine running and the car turned around by the time Alec and Steve made it back to the road. They leapt inside, and I threw the engine into gear and took off like the Devil himself was on my tail.

"Wh . . . what's wrong?" Alec gasped as soon as he caught his breath.

"I'm not sticking around at some creepy mansion with some glowing woman staring at me through the windows!" I said, speeding up the car in my agitation.

"A glowing woman!" Alec exclaimed.

"You mean you saw a ghost?" Steve asked.

"In the third-story window," I said, stomping even harder on the gas pedal. "What was that you and Alec were saying about keys?"

"We heard someone inside the mansion rattling keys and keeping pace with us as we walked along," Alec said. His voice sounded strange. I glanced over at him and realized that he was pale and shaking. "I thought they were Steve's keys rattling, and he thought they were mine."

"You said the mansion was abandoned," I said accusingly, slowing down a fraction to navigate the turn back onto the highway.

"It was. It is," said Alec.

"Except for a glowing woman and someone who rattles keys and crazy hunters on horseback," I replied sarcastically.

"Not to mention the killer nuns," Steve added from the back seat.

I let out a shriek and nearly crashed the car into the sedan in the next lane. "Killer nuns?"

Alec grabbed the wheel and pulled us back into our lane, steering until I got control of myself.

"Sure," Steve said, leaning forward between the two front seats and glancing from me to Alec. "Didn't Alec tell you about the crazy Mother Superior who became a pagan and tortured and killed her fellow sisters when they refused to join her evil practices? She chopped them up and scattered pieces of their bodies throughout the mansion. There was blood everywhere when the police came to investigate!"

"No, Alec failed to mention anything about killer nuns," I said stiffly. "I think I would have remembered *that* story."

"The Mother Superior's ghost is supposed to haunt the terraces at the back of the house. They say she tries to lead you into the mansion in order to torture and kill you," Steve explained.

"Does she rattle keys and appear in third-story windows?" I asked, my hands shaking on the wheel.

"I don't know," Steve admitted uncomfortably, leaning back against the rear seat.

"And I didn't want to wait around and find out," added Alec.

We drove the rest of the way in silence. I dropped off both of the fellows at Alec's place and then went home to a troubled sleep filled with the rattling keys and the glowing figure of a homicidal nun.

I found out later that the mansion was sold to a foundation and slated for restoration, along with the grounds. Several full-time staff members began living on the property. I wondered if any of them ever saw the glowing figure of a woman on the third story, but I never went back to ask.

8

Brotherly Love

SPRINGFIELD

My younger brother and I have been rivals since the day of his birth, a mere fourteen months after my own. When he wasn't taking the exact opposite point of view from me— usually in the loudest tone possible—he was trying to one-up my achievements. Naturally, as his older brother, I found these "endearing" traits very annoying and expressed a frequent desire to give the little twit the thrashing he deserved. I would have done it, too, except Ma wouldn't let me.

At first, it was little things that irked me. If Pa asked me to milk the cows and I got the chore done in record time, then the next day my L. B. (little brother) would beat my time by five minutes and boast about it for a week thereafter. If I decided to recite a sad poem in school, L. B. would choose a rollickingly funny poem that would have his class in stitches. I was an intellectual who got the best marks in school, so L. B. became a cutup who had to be forced to study. I built a tree house where I could read my books in peace; L. B. built a fortress where he and his friends could pretend to be frontiersmen conquering the Wild West. Do you see what I mean by a twit?

Unfortunately, L. B.'s contrary tendencies led him politically astray when he reached adulthood. As our nation started to fray around the debate over slavery, I backed the North's belief in freedom for all men. Within hours of my expressing this viewpoint, L. B. came out swinging for the South, claiming that the end of slavery would ruin that region's economy. He quoted a lot of political jargon that made me grit my teeth.

My parents were fair-minded folks. They didn't like L. B.'s viewpoint, but they respected his right to have his own opinion. None of us was really surprised when he left our Springfield home to join forces with General Robert E. Lee, once the real fighting started. When I left home to join up with the Yankee forces opposing them, Ma said to me, "Try not to kill your little brother, son. I'd prefer it if you both came home alive when all this is over."

I gave her a doubtful look and she chuckled, though she was a tad teary-eyed. "You've managed to refrain from killing him so far," she reminded me.

"Not from lack of inclination, I assure you," I replied. She and Pa laughed aloud, and that was how I remembered them during the long, brutal years of the war. I was injured just before it ended, so I missed the final months of conflict and the initial resolution. When I came to my senses, it was to discover that Lee had surrendered, Lincoln had been assassinated, and L. B. was safely home, covered with medals and glory for his service. He had spent much of his free time beside my bed. This would have been more touching if he had taken off his Confederate uniform.

"Well, B. B.," he said to me. (He had taken to calling me B. B.—big brother—within seconds of my calling him L. B.) "You Northerners won this round, but only by a whisker."

"That's what you think," I whispered weakly, sipping at the glass of water he held to my lips.

I didn't hear the whole story until some of my strength had returned. Lucky for him, L. B. was as saddened by Lincoln's assassination as the rest of us.

"A good man," was his assessment. "A bit misguided," he added with a sidelong look at me. "But a good man." Only respect for my mother kept me from assassinating L. B. for that gibe.

Our whole family turned out on Monday, April 24, 1865, to pay our respects to President Lincoln, whose body had been brought from Philadelphia to Jersey City on a funeral train called the Lincoln Special. His coffin was removed from the railroad car, taken by ferry across the Hudson River, driven down to New York City Hall, and carried up the circular staircase. Under the rotunda, it was placed on a black velvet dais. Respectful citizens waited in line for hours that day to say good-bye.

I broke down and cried when I viewed the face of the man for whom I had fought in that terrible war. L. B. steadied me as we slowly moved away, since I hardly had the strength to walk and my right arm was still in a sling. We stayed overnight with some friends in the city so that we could attend the funeral procession the next day.

Around 2:00 p.m., the president's coffin was placed on a magnificent funeral car drawn by sixteen horses wearing long blankets. The procession began on Broadway and ended at the Hudson River Railway Depot. The papers later estimated that nearly 75,000 citizens had marched through New York's packed streets, and I heard that windows along the route had rented for up to $100 a person.

Back in Springfield, L. B. stayed home only long enough to ensure my return to good health. Then he was gone, having moved to the next town to pursue a career and the pretty red-haired nurse who had looked after me when I was ill. The next thing I knew, he and I were both married with families of our own, and it was our sons who were trying to outdo one another. Our wives got along great, which was more than could be said for L. B. and me. Yet, one day our time came, and we were buried side by side in our family plot in Springfield.

Once in a while, I felt the need to come back and ponder life while floating over the places I had once called home. It wasn't that I didn't like heaven; I just wanted to see how things had changed.

The second time I returned to earth, I was musing upon the happy times I had had with my wife when L. B. suddenly turned up and sat down on his tombstone. I had returned in spirit form only, but not L. B. No, he was a full-blown apparition, glowing from the radiance that became a natural part of us once we entered the holy realm. He was dressed in his Confederate uniform and was even wearing his medals! Well, that was the final straw. I materialized in my resplendent Union uniform (also covered with medals), sat down on my tombstone, and glared at L. B.

"Must you follow me everywhere I go?" I demanded icily.

"Only when you go interesting places," L. B. replied jauntily.

"And why are you wearing that ridiculous uniform?" I asked. "You lost the war, remember?"

"We fought with courage and honor!" L. B. retorted. "And President Lincoln himself said that the North and the South were to be friends, in his speech at Gettysburg. At least I think that's where he said it."

BROTHERLY LOVE

"You never can remember things correctly!" I shouted, jumping up and shaking my finger at him. "It was at his first inaugural address on March 4, 1861, that President Lincoln said, 'We are not enemies, but friends. We must not be enemies. Though passion may have strained, it must not break our bonds of affection. The mystic chords of memory, stretching from every battlefield and patriot grave to every living heart and hearthstone all over this broad land, will yet swell the chorus of the Union, when again touched, as surely they will be, by the better angels of our nature.'"

The meaning of the words hit me suddenly, and I sat down rather abruptly on my tombstone, staring at my lifelong enemy, at my friend, at my little brother.

It was at this interesting juncture that a young man dressed in a rather rumpled suit and carrying a bottle in a brown bag came staggering toward us. His mouth hung open in amazement at the sight of two arguing ghosts. L. B. and I looked at each other and then at the man. Suddenly, we both leapt to our feet and shouted "Boo!" as loudly as we could. The drunken fellow gave a shriek of terror and ran away so fast that he left his bottle behind.

L. B. and I hooted with laughter. Then L. B. picked up the bottle and looked at it meditatively.

"I wouldn't drink that if I were you," I said. "You don't know where it's been."

"So what? Do you think it will kill me?" asked the ghost of my brother.

"If it doesn't, I might," I replied.

We grinned at each other, for once in complete harmony. Then we disappeared, leaving the graveyard to rest in its rather solemn peace.

9

The Girl in the Mirror

CAPE MAY

"Have you ever seen a ghost, Grandpa?" seven-year-old Lisa asked my husband, Joe, as they sat on low stools on the front walk, weeding the flower beds together.

"Yep," said my husband of forty-one years laconically. Lisa's eyes grew large and she shoved her golden hair back with a dirty hand, leaving a muddy streak on her freckled cheek.

"You have?" she asked breathlessly.

"I saw one once," said Joe, giving me a mischievous sideways glance and the debonair grin that had won my heart so many years ago. I caught my breath, partly because Joe was still the handsomest rascal I had ever seen and partly because I knew what he was going to say next. "But your grandma has seen a couple of ghosts."

"Now, Joe," I said in a reproachful tone from my seat on the porch steps.

"Now, Lilly," he mimicked.

Lisa whirled around to look at me. "Grandma has seen ghosts?" she cried, obviously thrilled with the idea.

"Tell Lisa about our trip to Cape May," Joe said. "We went there on a weekend getaway for our fortieth anniversary, and we stayed in a haunted house!"

It was obvious that no more weeding was going to be done until I told my story. I handed out the lemonade waiting for us on the wicker table next to the porch swing and began my tale as we sipped its cool sweetness.

"Well, your grandpa booked us into a luxury bed-and-breakfast in the heart of historic Cape May. It was an absolutely beautiful Italianate mansion built around 1860, with lovely gardens, luxurious rooms, and amazing food. The property is surrounded by a 150-year-old hedgerow, which makes a convenient barrier between the bustling streets of old Cape May and the peaceful atmosphere of the inn."

"You sound like a brochure, Lilly," Joe said teasingly. "Cut to the chase and tell Lisa about the ghost!"

I gave Joe a mocking glare and told him to hush. Then I related the following story.

We checked into the inn on Friday afternoon and soon were unpacking our suitcases in the master suite that Joe had booked for the "honeymooners." It was furnished with beautiful antiques and featured a huge, fancy bed; a large wardrobe with a full-length mirror in it; a fireplace with a red sofa beside it; a bathroom with a claw-foot tub; and a lovely sunporch. As I stood brushing my hair in front of the mirror, I caught a whiff of expensive perfume. For a moment I felt as if someone—a woman—was staring at me from the doorway to the suite, which was strange because the door was closed.

"Joe?" I called, even though I knew he had stepped out onto the sunporch.

Joe reappeared, swept me into his arms, and waltzed me all around the room. "Some place, eh?" he said, giving me a kiss.

"Some place," I agreed, and followed him out of the suite. We went to a romantic restaurant in town for dinner, returning quite late. As we walked down the hallway on our way to the suite, I happened to glance into one of the ornate mirrors on the wall and saw the reflection of a pretty woman in a long gown. She smiled at me, and I caught a whiff of the same perfume I had smelled earlier. I turned around to look at the woman, but there was no one there! I looked back into the mirror and saw the woman giggling at my confusion. Again, I whirled around, but there was still no one standing where the reflection indicated the woman should be. My heart throbbed and my skin prickled superstitiously.

"What are you looking at, Lilly?" asked Joe, who had forged ahead while I was staring into the glass. The girl in the mirror disappeared as soon as Joe joined me.

"I thought I saw something," I said weakly. I was shaking with astonishment, but I felt no fear. The girl's face had been too friendly and full of life for me to be afraid of her. As we entered our room, I thought I heard the rustle of long skirts— as if a young woman was hurrying back the way we had just come.

In spite of my uncanny experience, I slept soundly in the beautiful room. The next morning I stood in front of the big mirror trying to decide between two outfits. Suddenly, the friendly girl in the old-fashioned gown appeared in the mirror. She was standing behind me, next to the bed. When she saw the dress I held in front of me, she shook her head and pointed to the one I had left on the covers. Just then, Joe called out something from the bathroom, and the girl disappeared. Hastily, I donned the dress draped on the bed and went to take Joe his razor.

"You look wonderful, honey," he said, giving me a kiss full of shaving cream.

After a delicious breakfast, we spent the morning exploring the mansion and grounds. Joe chased me up and down an ornate spiral staircase, trying to tickle the backs of my knees, and later he waltzed me around one of the elegant ballrooms. I caught a glimpse of the girl in some of the mirrors as we whirled about. She was dancing gracefully, but she had no partner. I waved to her and saw her wave back as Joe took me through an elaborate turn. Later, we walked hand in hand through the gardens and then sat for a while on the veranda, sipping iced tea.

I grew used to the odd glimpses I caught of the girl whenever I walked past a mirror. She seemed fascinated by me and Joe; it felt like I was being spied upon by a happy-go-lucky younger sister. At one point Joe remarked that he liked the smell of the perfume I was wearing. Not sure how he would respond to the notion of a ghost, I didn't tell him that it was not my perfume he smelled.

We spent the afternoon on the beach and enjoyed another lovely dinner. It was our last night at the inn. As we walked to our room, I caught another glimpse of the girl. She smiled at us from the same mirror in which I had first seen her. This time Joe saw her, too.

"Look, Lilly!" he said. "They must be having a costume ball."

He turned around to look at the girl, then snapped his eyes back to me when confronted with an empty hallway.

"Where did she go?" he asked in confusion. In the mirror the girl started to giggle, and I grinned at her.

THE GIRL IN THE MIRROR

"She's right there," I said calmly, pointing to the mirror. Joe stared at her in astonishment, looking first into the mirror and then back to the empty spot where the girl should have been standing.

"This is some sort of joke, right?" he asked cautiously.

"No joke, dear. Just a ghost," I said.

The girl waved to Joe in the mirror and curtsied. We both heard the rustle of her skirts as she moved. The smell of expensive perfume filled the hallway as she disappeared.

"Okay, that's enough of the paranormal for one day," Joe said rather hastily. He escorted me into our bedroom and deliberately covered the mirror on the wardrobe with a blanket before we went to bed. I thought I heard a faint laugh from the direction of the covered mirror just before he put out the lights.

We checked out of the hotel the next morning. As we walked one last time through the handsome rooms, I caught a glimpse of the girl watching us from an ornate mirror in the entrance. I waved to her and she smiled. Joe saw my gesture from the corner of his eye. He looked into the mirror, gave the girl a cordial nod, and then swept us out the door and away from that lovely, haunted mansion.

I finished my story and my lemonade at the same time and rose to my feet.

"Now, why don't we finish weeding the front garden before it gets too hot?" I proposed.

"Aw, Grandma," Lisa groaned, but she handed me her glass and stood up.

"Do you think other people have seen the ghost?" she asked as Joe swung her off the steps, whirled her about, and then put her on the sidewalk beside her weeding stool.

"I asked the owners about it," I said. "Apparently, we aren't the only ones who have seen the girl in the mirror or smelled her perfume. They call her Esther, and they think she might be the niece of the man who built the mansion back in the 1860s."

"The ghost of Esther," Lisa said. "I like it. Maybe Mom and Dad and I can go stay at the inn in Cape May sometime."

"Maybe," I replied with a smile. Then I shooed my husband and granddaughter back to their weeding and went to wash our empty glasses in the kitchen sink.

10

The Sweet By and By

BARNEGAT LIGHT

Matilda held her baby daughter close to her chest, humming softly as the hold of the ship swayed and rattled and shook in the terrible storm.

"In the sweet by and by, we shall meet on that beautiful shore," she whisper-sang against her baby's silky soft hair, knowing how impossible it was to hear in the roaring noise belowdecks, but hoping something of the tune or rhythm or perhaps just the buzzing hum would calm the fretful infant. Not that Matilda blamed the baby for crying. After three days of sailing through the winter storm-swept sea, she felt like crying herself. Her stomach would hold no food, and even when she was lying on the bed in the small captain's cabin, she could barely keep her balance as the ship rolled from side to side.

Matilda had barely seen her husband, the captain, since the howling storm had begun. He and his crew were doing everything they could to keep the iron-hulled schooner from sinking into the ocean. They had invested all of their money in this voyage, and her husband was determined that their journey would not fail. She just prayed that everything he was doing to keep them afloat would be enough. By this time Matilda didn't care about the ship, so long as they survived the storm with their lives.

"In the sweet by and by, we shall meet on that beautiful shore." Matilda crooned the words of the Samuel Bennett song again, to comfort herself as much as the baby.

Suddenly the ship gave a terrible jolt and shook from stem to stern, throwing mother and baby off the bed. Matilda cradled the infant tightly, managing to twist around so that the baby was not injured in their fall. The swaying of the ship was different now. It rocked violently backward and forward as if it was somehow beached and the waves were trying to knock it over. Matilda was terrified, realizing that they must have run aground. The ship would be torn to pieces!

Matilda could hear the sailors shouting outside, their voices rising above the thunderous roar of the wind and sleet and rain. She crouched on the floor, sliding from one side to the other as the ship tilted. She did not dare rise, knowing she would fall immediately and not wanting to risk any injury to her daughter. The little baby was screaming now, so Matilda started singing again, even though her throat was so tight she could barely breathe and her heart thundered in her chest.

> *There's a land that is fairer than day*
> *And by faith we can see it afar;*
> *For the Father waits over the way*
> *To prepare us a dwelling place there.*
> *In the sweet by and by*
> *We shall meet on that beautiful shore.*
> *In the sweet by and by*
> *We shall meet on that beautiful shore.*

The door to the cabin burst open and the captain staggered in, grasping the doorframe tightly to retain his balance.

"We've struck ground, but it's all right," he shouted. "The lifesavers on the beach have fired a grappling hook, and we've got it secured against the side of the ship. They're sending an iron life-car out for the crew. You and the baby will go ashore on the first trip."

He helped Matilda to her feet and tenderly wrapped her and the baby in a winter cloak to keep them warm against the frigid air outside. Then, holding them tightly with one arm and clutching the wall for balance with the other, he slid them carefully through the cabin door. The first mate leapt up the icy, tilted deck to help the captain steady mother and daughter, and the other sailors pulled a long iron tube toward the ship. When it reached the side, the captain urged his wife to get in.

"What about you?" Matilda asked. She knew her husband well. Something in his manner told her that he was keeping a secret.

"I will stay here until the crew has been evacuated," he hedged, trying to lift her into the lifeboat. Matilda resisted, glaring at him through the roaring wind and sleet.

"And then you are coming ashore," she demanded.

He nodded, not meeting her eyes, and Matilda knew immediately that he was lying. Everything they possessed was on this ship, and all their money was sunk into the cargo. If the ship went down, they lost everything. If by a miracle the ship survived the storm, the first person to tow her into harbor would be able to claim the ship and all she contained by right of salvage. The captain would never let that happen. The ship had an iron hull, so it had a better chance than most of surviving. Knowing this, he had elected to stay aboard and try to salvage what he could after the storm. If that failed, he would go down with the ship.

Turning, Matilda thrust the baby into the first mate's arms. "Take her," she commanded fiercely. "Take her to shore and keep her safe. Her father and I will come for her after the storm. Only pray that we do not drown."

The first mate protested violently, but seeing the look in her eyes, he took the baby. The captain swore and shouted and tried to lift his wife into the rescue boat, but she fought him fiercely.

"I won't leave you. I won't!" Matilda shouted back.

The second mate gestured to the first mate to get aboard the lifeboat. They did not have time to interfere in this argument; the crew needed to get off the storm-tossed ship as soon as possible. And so while husband and wife raged at one another, the crew evacuated. Finally, the captain tore at his thinning hair in dismay and agreed to let Matilda stay.

After everyone else had departed, the couple lashed themselves with rope to the main mast as best they could, entrusting their lives to the mercy of God. They held each other close as the grounded ship was buffeted back and forth, back and forth by the huge waves.

Once ashore, the first mate found a local couple that lived nearby to care for the infant while he helped with the rescue efforts. Even after all of the crew was safely on land, he remained on the beach, huddled under several blankets that the thoughtful islanders had given him, watching the ship where the captain and his wife waited out the storm. It was bitterly cold. The men of the island urged him to take shelter and stay warm by the fire, but the first mate kept returning to the beach every hour or so to look out to sea at the ship he had left behind.

THE SWEET BY AND BY

To his surprise and joy, when the storm finally blew itself out, the battered ship was still intact. He and several fishermen rowed out as soon as it was safe, and the first mate sprang aboard, calling out to his captain. There was no answer. It took but a moment for him to locate the couple lashed to the main mast. They were locked in each other's arms, their heads resting tenderly against one another. They had frozen to death during the fierce winter storm.

The big, burly first mate broke down and wept when he saw them, and even the tough island fishermen sniffled as they carefully cut the captain and his wife down from their perch.

The couple was buried on the island, and their tiny daughter was adopted by the kind people who had cared for her the night of the shipwreck. The husband was one of the fishermen who had returned to the ship with the first mate after the storm. Every night he would take the baby on his knee and tell her about her brave parents, who loved her so much that they sent her to safety while they stayed with their vessel.

Two weeks after the wreck, another winter storm blew in during the early evening. The loud roar of thunder woke the baby, who had just been put to bed. The infant started wailing, and the fisherman instantly put aside his book and ran upstairs. As he descended the steps a few moments later, his besotted eyes fixed on the mite in his arms, the fisherman's wife shook her head and smiled. Then she went to the kitchen to fix a bottle while the fisherman rocked the baby tenderly, humming the tune of "The Sweet By and By." The first mate had told him that it was the lullaby the infant's parents had used to get her to sleep at night.

Suddenly, from outside the rain-lashed window, the fisherman heard two voices joining him in the first verse of the hymn.

There's a land that is fairer than day
And by faith we can see it afar;
For the Father waits over the way
To prepare us a dwelling place there.

The fisherman went to the window and looked outside. Strolling down the road in front of his house was a handsome couple wearing heavy coats, winter scarves, gloves, and hats. They were walking hand in hand and singing together, seemingly oblivious to the brutal wind and lashing rain. They carried no lantern, and yet they were bathed with a heavenly light that seemed to glow from their faces and clothing. Their feet did not touch the ground. The fisherman recognized them at once: It was the frozen sea captain and his wife. They paused in front of the house and sang the second verse of the song.

We shall sing on that beautiful shore
The melodious songs of the blest,
And our spirits shall sorrow no more
Not a sigh for the blessing of rest.

In the fisherman's arms, the baby stopped crying as she listened to her parents' voices. Behind him, the fisherman could hear his wife in the kitchen, singing along with the chorus.

The glowing couple gazed longingly up at the house, and the fisherman held their baby up to the window so that they could see her. The infant cooed and waved a tiny fist as if in greeting. The captain and his wife waved back, and Matilda mouthed the words "thank you" to the kind fisherman. Then they were gone.

"You've got her calmed down," said the fisherman's wife, reentering the parlor with a bottle in her hand.

He blinked away tears and handed the baby to his wife. "That's the song her parents always sang to her," he told her gruffly.

"Then we must sing it to her as well, in remembrance of them," said his wife.

"In remembrance," he echoed, glancing out the window at the now-empty road. He pondered on the appropriateness of the song the couple had chosen for the child's lullaby. In his heart, he was sure that one day the parents and their daughter *would* meet again.

In the sweet by and by
We shall meet on that beautiful shore.
In the sweet by and by
We shall meet on that beautiful shore.

11

The Ghost in the Storm

MORRISTOWN

It was a bitterly cold day, and the air was heavy with the threat of snow. I swept off the front steps carefully and chipped away at the frozen puddle that had formed when icicles on the eaves had started to melt. I didn't expect many customers to visit the tavern on such a miserable day, but the chores still needed to be done.

Once the steps were clear, I went inside to polish the glasses and make sure the bar was sparkling. Outside, I heard the wind pick up. By the time the first of the evening's customers blew into Arnold's Tavern, it was snowing.

"Horrible weather we're having," called old Nate Taylor, a large, red-faced man who took a seat at the bar with two friends.

"Worst winter in years," I agreed. "Not so bad for us working men, but it is really hard on General Washington's troops. My wife is constantly knitting scarves and socks and whatnot to take up to the boys in Jockey Hollow."

I set drinks in front of Nate and his buddies.

"My wife's up half the night sewing clothes and blankets. We have a boy with the New Jersey Militia," said Henry, the owner of the mercantile, looking grave. "He's been lucky so far—survived both the battle at Trenton and the action down in Princeton."

"I hear that Washington has ordered his Continentals and the New Jersey Militia to engage enemy outposts," Nate said. "Wants to contain the British by harassing and tiring them with constant patrols."

"That's what he says," I agreed.

General Washington had been using Arnold's Tavern as his headquarters since he came to Morristown, after the British drove the Continental Army out of New York. I had come to know and respect the General during the long winter.

After fighting the British to a standstill at White Plains, General Washington had moved most of his army south into New Jersey, reasoning that the British would soon try to take control of Philadelphia, as they had just done in New York City. The British general, Cornwallis, had started attacking the Continentals as soon as they arrived in New Jersey. Things looked pretty grim for Washington and his men.

Then Howe ordered the British army into winter quarters, and Washington seized his chance. The Continentals attacked the British twice—once at Trenton in December 1776 and once at Princeton in January 1777—and won both battles. Folks here in Morristown had started questioning Washington's fitness to lead the troops after his defeat in New York, but the two New Jersey victories helped put a lot of speculation to rest. I didn't agree with the talk and was glad when it died down. My wife's parents were Tories, but the missus and I were staunch believers in freedom from Britain. I was glad to serve the war effort, even if the most I could do with my arthritic legs was to serve General Washington drinks on the house.

The General was continually telling me that the militia had problems finding new recruits and that many men had already deserted. The British also suffered from desertions, but they were actively enlisting as many of our countrymen as they could seduce with their promises. Our militia and the enemy's foraging parties had frequent skirmishes in which the British usually sustained greater losses in killed and wounded, owing to the superior skill of our boys in the use of firearms.

The storm outside was getting worse. Nate and his buddies finished their drinks, wrapped up tight against the weather, and went home. The tavern was empty, and I wasn't expecting to see anyone else that night. However, two hours later the General himself staggered in, accompanied by his driver. He was half-frozen; I hurried to help him out of his soaking outer garments, then settled him into a chair with a drink. The missus had heard him arrive, and she soon entered the tavern with plates full of food, which the General and his driver ate with gratitude.

By this time, I knew the General well enough to know there was something bothering him besides the cold weather. I did not ask any questions, just kept him supplied with drinks and food. Several of his soldiers came into the bar to speak with him, but he quickly dismissed them and, later, his driver. When we were alone, Washington sat back in his chair and studied me closely. "Do you believe in ghosts?" he asked me point-blank.

I blinked, finding the question unexpected. Did I believe in ghosts? I had never seen one, but my wife often complained that her grandmother's ghost stole the clothespins out of her laundry basket and used them to entertain the baby when the child was supposed to be taking a nap. Since the old lady in question had undoubtedly done this in life, I was not surprised that she continued to do so after death.

"Yes, I do believe in ghosts," I said cautiously. "Why do you ask?"

The General stirred uneasily and looked down at his plate. "We were driving back to Morristown from Summit when the blizzard came blowing down upon our carriage," he finally said. "It was difficult to see, but as we continued slowly down the road, I looked through the window and glimpsed a poor child—a pretty little brown-haired girl—staggering through the rapidly deepening drifts. I called to my driver to stop and pick her up; I thought we could take her home. But just as the driver got down from the carriage, she vanished—disappeared into thin air. When we looked around for her, we realized there were no footprints in the snow!"

I gasped in astonishment. The General nodded solemnly, then continued: "We stopped at the next house to inquire after the girl, not ready to believe we had seen a phantom. The woman at the house knew instantly of whom we spoke. The little girl drowned in a cistern several years ago, and her ghost continues to walk the section of the road on which we traveled this night. It is said that the little girl has sometimes saved other children from similar accidents, and that her spirit is there to protect travelers."

"Did you need protecting?" I asked him.

"I do not know," the General said. "As we left, the young son of the house ran in from the yard to tell his mother that some of the local men had just captured several British soldiers who were raiding the nearby settlement. The soldiers were located only a half mile down the road from where we stopped.

THE GHOST IN THE STORM

If we had not seen the little girl's ghost, we would have driven right into the midst of them, with unknown consequences."

The General drained his glass and set it down. "Let's just say I am thankful to be alive this night." He rose, stretched, and bid me good night.

As I locked up the tavern, I mused upon the General's story. Whoever the phantom girl was, I was grateful to her for halting the General's carriage before it ran into the British raiders. I had a feeling that Washington was going to be a key player in this war against the British. We couldn't afford to lose him.

Picking up the General's plate and glass, I carried them into the kitchen and went to tell my wife about the ghost in the storm.

12

Turnabout Is Fair Play

BRANCHVILLE

Old Uncle Phil was a tall scarecrow of a fellow who was jumpier than a grasshopper. He lived and worked on a small farm near Branchville, and he believed that the hostile world was largely populated with monsters and ghosts and spooks and witches and werewolves. Uncle Phil believed in just about every sort of scary critter that you can imagine. He shied away from shadows, jumped whenever anyone spoke to him, and lived in perpetual fear that someone, somewhere, was out to get him.

Uncle Phil wore so many amulets that he chimed and rattled and clanked whenever he moved. Early in life, he took a trip to Pennsylvania Dutch Country to learn what the most powerful hex signs were so he could paint them on his house and barn. He even planted a special garden around his house that was full of trees and bushes and plants designed to thwart the forces of evil.

Uncle Phil hated to go outside after dark. He always carried a lantern with him so as not to be caught anywhere without light. He even took the long way home rather than walk through the "ominous" woods surrounding the river. He became so paranoid that he refused to shake hands with anyone because it might allow an evil spirit to enter him, and he never entered a house that had a cat, because he thought that the animal might be an imp or a witch's familiar.

Naturally, this attitude made Uncle Phil the butt of many jokes. Children in particular took a rather cruel delight in plaguing the old man. At first it was just small things, like stealing the apples from his orchard, tossing rocks into his path from behind trees, or tapping his shoulder when he was buying groceries in the store. The youngsters would howl with laughter when Uncle Phil yelped and whirled around, and they giggled and whispered whenever he complained about the goblins who stole all his apples away.

One summer a new family moved to town with two sons who were very naughty indeed. As soon as they learned about jumpy Uncle Phil, those boys became obsessed with tormenting him. They snuck out to his place one night and painted over all his hex signs. When Uncle Phil woke up the next morning, the barn and the house were bare. He ran all the way to town on foot—forgetting that he owned a horse—because he was sure the Devil had removed the hex signs in order to steal his soul away while he slept. The old man crouched in a pew in the local church and wouldn't leave until the minister had prayed over his house and the neighborhood painter had re-created the hex signs.

A week after this event, the boys gathered all of the black cats in town and put them into Uncle Phil's house while he was away. When Uncle Phil opened the door, his dog rushed into the front room; fur started flying everywhere as the black cats hissed and scratched and yowled and bit. Back ran Uncle Phil to the church, and back came the minister with some helpers to clear the house of black cats and bless it against any evil witches who wanted to curse Uncle Phil.

The boys were forced to lay low for a while after this incident, which had upset all the adults in town. The schoolchildren were subjected to a lecture on cruelty and instructed to report any mischief committed against Uncle Phil. Of course all the children knew who the culprits were, but no one told.

For a month Uncle Phil was left in peace. No fruit disappeared from his orchards, no mysterious ghost tapped his shoulder, no goblins tossed rocks at him from the trees. Then the boys came up with another plan. One night, they snuck into Uncle Phil's house through the parlor window, dragging a scarecrow inside with them. They set up the scarecrow so that it loomed over the poor sleeping man with one arm outthrust, as if it wanted to shake hands with him. Then they positioned a lantern on a tree branch just outside the second-story room so that the light illuminated the scarecrow's grotesque face. Once everything was in place, the boys started moaning and groaning and calling Uncle Phil's name from the yard outside his bedroom window.

Uncle Phil woke with a gasp and then screamed in sheer terror when his eyes encountered the scarecrow. Leaping off the bed, he dove out of his bedroom window and climbed to the very top of the tree. From his high perch Uncle Phil clutched desperately at the various charms he wore under his nightshirt and said the Twenty-third Psalm aloud. Below him the lantern rocked dangerously and then fell to the ground, setting fire to the woodpile beside the house. The boys stopped laughing when they realized that Uncle Phil's house was on fire. They ran to the barn and wet some old sacks in the water barrel. Together, they managed to put out the fire, but not before the

TURNABOUT IS FAIR PLAY

whole side of the house was scorched. In the tree above them, they could hear Uncle Phil begging God to spare him from the terrible devil who had come with his grotesque face and his flames to take Uncle Phil's soul.

Afraid of what their parents would do if they discovered the trick, the boys snuck into the house and removed the scarecrow before hightailing it home. In the morning Uncle Phil came down from the top of the tree and went to fetch the preacher. The minister and many of the leading citizens in town were amazed when they saw the huge scorch mark on the side of Uncle Phil's house where—he claimed—the Devil had come and tried to take away his soul.

Uncle Phil shivered and shook all morning as people came to inspect his house. He was still dressed in his nightshirt because he refused to go back inside to change. Finally, the minister's wife took Uncle Phil home with her and tucked him into bed with a bowl of hot soup. The minister had to perform a third ritual cleansing of the farm before Uncle Phil would return to his property.

The boys were afraid to play any more pranks after their last escapade ended so dramatically. Life went back to normal for Uncle Phil—at least, as normal as it could be for someone who believed in ghosts and goblins and witches and werewolves and all sorts of crazy critters. Then, about a month after the "Devil's visit," Uncle Phil passed away in his sleep. The whole town turned out for his funeral, and many folks were saddened that such a colorful figure had left their lives.

The boys felt terrible about the old man's death, afraid that their trick with the scarecrow might have weakened him and caused his final passing. But they were scared to confess that they were the ones who had played the trick on Uncle Phil. They grew very quiet in school and did their chores listlessly at home. Their mother was so worried by their lack of spirit that she started treating them with cod-liver oil and mustard plasters. Nothing helped.

Two weeks after Uncle Phil's death, the boys woke to find their bedroom full of black cats. The boys shouted in alarm, which made the cats hiss and scratch and yowl and bite. Their parents came running into the room and were furious at the scene. The boys could not convince them that they did not know how the cats got there.

A week passed. When the boys came home from school one afternoon, they saw that a hex sign had been painted on their barn—the very same sign that they had painted over on Uncle Phil's barn. The boys let out a yell of terror and ran inside their house, pulling their mother away from her bread dough to look at the barn. But when they reached the far wall, the hex sign was gone.

For the next several days, the boys were tormented by an unseen foe. Rotten fruit would pelt them as they walked through the woods. Someone would tap their shoulders in the schoolyard, causing them to yelp and whirl around, only to find that no one was there. After dark the boys would hear the chiming and clanking sound of amulets as they walked along the shadowy lanes near their home.

One night, the boys woke to hear a voice moaning their names over and over again. They sat up in their beds and lit the lantern, which illuminated a grotesque scarecrow looming in the center of the room. The boys screamed in terror, and the younger lad leapt into bed with his brother as the scarecrow started to move toward them. "I have come for your soul," it moaned, waving its arms about.

Then the scarecrow started laughing. It shook a finger at the cowering boys, and they heard the chiming and clanking of amulets. One arm reached up and snatched off the scarecrow's head, revealing the glowing, partially transparent face of Uncle Phil.

"Gotcha!" said the ghost of Uncle Phil with a huge grin. Then he disappeared.

The boys were torn between abject terror and amusement. They clung together, alternating between laughing and crying until their parents came in to see what was causing all the ruckus. The teary-eyed boys told their parents the whole story, starting with the tricks they had played on Uncle Phil and ending with the pranks his ghost had pulled on them. They pointed out the wisps of hay on the floor and the painted sack that the ghost had used as a scarecrow's head.

When the boys finished their story, their father sat back against the wall and started to laugh heartily. "It serves you right," he said. "After all, turnabout is fair play!"

The boys had to agree with him. After that they stuck to their games and school rivalries and never played another practical joke again.

13

Apples and Oranges

BORDENTOWN

I finished lacing my skates and headed onto the ice of the local pond. It was a crisp, clear winter day with an endlessly blue sky and just a few wisps of pure white cloud to compete with the snowy ground. Absolutely lovely. I drew in a deep breath of chilly air and commenced skating with a fairly competent figure eight.

The kids were already out on the ice, laughing and skating in circles, tugging at one another and shouting loudly. They were, I knew, trying to attract the attention of the ghost of Joseph Bonaparte, the onetime king of Spain who now haunted this place. I wasn't sure if it would work; by all reports, the ghost usually appeared at dusk. But they were lucky today. As I watched their cavorting from a safe distance, an apple rolled onto the ice, right to the foot of my nephew. He gave a shout and bent to pick it up, only to have it disappear just before his hand reached it.

"Me too, me too," my niece cried excitedly, waving in the direction from which the apple had been thrown. Before the words had left her mouth, she was bonked on the head by an orange that bounced away across the ice. Laughing, she gave chase, but the orange disappeared after a few feet. Rubbing her head dramatically, she skated over to me and plopped down on the ice.

"Why does he do it?" she asked as another apple rolled toward us. I grinned, lunged for the apple, and toppled to the ice beside her in triumph, the apple clutched in my hand for a moment. It vanished before our eyes as my nephew joined us, sliding to a seat.

"It's just a game that the ghost likes to play. When he was alive, Joseph Bonaparte used to encourage the local townsfolk to come skate on his pond by rolling fresh apples and oranges from his greenhouses out to them. Back then, during the winter folks mostly ate old apples they had stored in their cellars or preserved in jams and jellies. Oranges were even rarer, since they came only with the big trading ships. So having the former king of Spain give them fresh fruit from his greenhouse was a big treat, and because he did it in such a playful way, he did not insult anyone's pride with his generosity."

"Was he really the brother of Napoleon Bonaparte?" asked my niece, wide-eyed. She had just studied the French Revolution and its aftermath in school.

I nodded with a grin.

"What was he doing in New Jersey?" asked my nephew.

"Living here, of course. Just like you and me," I replied, and told them the following story.

Joseph Bonaparte was placed on the throne of Naples and then Spain by his famous brother, Napoleon. Unsuccessful in defending Spain against England during the Peninsular Wars, Joseph was forced to abdicate the throne in 1813. He went into exile in America after Napoleon's eventual defeat.

APPLES AND ORANGES

At first the ex-king tried to settle in Pennsylvania, but they wouldn't sell land to a foreigner, even a royal one, and Joseph refused to apply for American citizenship. The folks in New Jersey were more generous: They passed a special act that allowed Joseph to purchase 800 acres at Point Breeze in Bordentown. Joseph claimed that once, while he and his brother were studying a map, Napoleon had pointed to this place and said that if ever he were forced into exile, he would live halfway between the great seaports of New York and Philadelphia. From that location he could obtain the very latest news from France and Spain. So Joseph took his infamous brother's advice.

As befitting royalty (even the dethroned sort), Joseph built himself a lovely mansion with beautiful, landscaped grounds and plenty of parkland. Joseph was afraid that Spanish or French patriots might try to assassinate him, so he had escape tunnels built underneath the property. These tunnels led out to the river and the road, and to a few connected buildings on the property.

Joseph started entertaining many of the great men of his day: President John Adams, the Marquis de Lafayette, and statesman Daniel Webster all visited the nobleman's mansion during his stay in America. During this time many Frenchmen also came to see the former king, and their presence sparked a strange story in the local community—namely, that these ex-patriots had smuggled Napoleon himself into America after spreading rumors that the emperor had died on St. Helena. No one ever saw Napoleon with their own eyes, though.

Joseph had a string of beautiful young mistresses while he lived in America (the rather unpleasant Mistress Bonaparte had decided to remain in Europe rather than go into exile with him). He led a very glamorous social life, throwing marvelous parties with mountains of food and many guests. The Americans were very impressed with the former king, and he with them. When his mansion burned to the ground, his neighbors actually helped carry out the salvageable furniture and paintings and a chest of gold coins. Joseph was astonished. If he had been in France in similar conditions, the gold coins—and quite possibly the expensive furnishings—would have been stolen.

Once things settled down in Europe, Joseph went to Florence, Italy, to rejoin his wife; he remained there until his death in 1844. They say that people in Point Breeze sometimes still hear the rattle and clink of cutlery, the murmur of voices punctuated by laughter, and the faint sound of music coming from underneath their feet. Perhaps a few leftover party guests are still roaming the tunnels.

The property now houses the Divine World Missionaries rather than a former king. And the tunnels have been blocked or closed after many years of disuse. But the ghost of Joseph Bonaparte still comes to his former parkland to play games with people skating on the pond.

As I finished my story, another orange rolled across the ice and bumped into my right skate. The three of us looked up. For just an instant, I saw a sketchy, elegant figure in the beautifully cut formal clothing of another era smiling at us from the shore. I waved, and Joseph—if that's who it was—bowed graciously and vanished from view. I reached out and touched the skin of the orange with one finger. It felt cold and solid but vanished when I attempted to grasp it. I brought my finger away and lifted it to my nose; it smelled of orange.

"Come on," I exclaimed, rising to my feet and pulling up my niece and nephew. "I'll race you to the far side of the pond."

I set off immediately, and the kids shrieked in delight and followed at once. Behind us a few more apples skimmed the surface of the pond. I thought I heard a whisper of elegant music in the distance. Then it was gone.

14

Father and Son

I paged through a science book left on the instructor's desk, marveling at all the wonderful technologies that had been invented since my unfortunate demise at the age of forty-two, in the year of our Lord 1747. This personal tragedy had occurred shortly after I, Aaron Burr, the second president of the College of New Jersey, had moved the institution to Princeton. Anyone peering inside the classroom at that moment would have been startled by the sight of the pages of the book turning by themselves, since I had not materialized to do my reading. But I had been very careful to make sure I was alone before commencing my studies.

I thought the steam engine had been a marvelous invention, but clever Americans had followed it up with the telegraph, the telegram, the telephone, the automobile, the airplane, and computers. There is something called the Internet that seems to fascinate people of all ages, keeping them glued to their screens and keyboards long into the night. Apparently, they use it to communicate information to one another.

My reading was interrupted by the sound of squealing coming through the open window. I sighed and marked my place in the book. I was very familiar with that sound.

"Charlie, you are such a chauvinist!" a voice shouted from the walkway outside. I strolled to the window and observed a group of female students confronting a blushing boy of about nineteen years.

"I didn't do anything," he protested.

"Right," snapped a willowy brunette. "How would you like it if we pinched you?"

Charlie very rightly did not answer the question; he merely continued to protest his innocence.

Standing on the lawn not far away, the phantom of my son—Aaron Burr the second—was chuckling to himself and smirking at the pretty girls. I sighed. I had not known Aaron in life, having died when he was an infant, but I had gotten to know him too well in the afterlife, especially since he had taken to haunting my university. And what a son he was. He had been the second vice president of the United States, the governor of New York, and a senator. But he was also an alleged traitor, a womanizer, and the killer of Alexander Hamilton. In my opinion his bad parts far outweighed the good. We were buried side by side in a Princeton cemetery, and since that day his ghost had wandered about the place, causing me grief.

I materialized beside my son. "That was not well done," I remarked, gesturing to the blushing Charlie, who was creeping away with his ears still ringing from the brunette's lecture.

"On the contrary, it was very well done indeed," my son said with a wicked smile. "I got all the fun and Charlie got all the blame. What more could I ask for? I am so delighted that the university finally went 'coed.' It makes the afterlife so much more interesting, don't you think?"

FATHER AND SON

"Someday, you will get your comeuppance," I retorted. "These Princeton ladies are smart. None of these girls would ever have fallen for an inveterate womanizer like you. Go behave yourself."

"I'll go, but I won't promise the good behavior," my son replied.

He vanished and I returned to the classroom and to my studies. But I could not stop thinking about my son. He had inherited money from my estate and graduated from the College of New Jersey at the tender age of sixteen. Aaron was a bright lad and ambitious. He served well in the American Revolution, starting out under the command of Benedict Arnold, who betrayed the Republic, and later serving with Washington, with whom he did not get along.

Aaron started his political career as a delegate to the New York Congress, and in 1782 he was admitted to the state bar. He was a very successful lawyer and made a good deal of money. Unfortunately, he enjoyed the trappings of wealth—handsome carriages, well-appointed residences, elegant clothing, lavish entertaining—and often lived beyond his means. He spent much of his life heavily in debt.

Aaron became a political rival of another lawyer, a man called Alexander Hamilton, who was a friend of George Washington. Hamilton was one of the writers of the Federalist essays, which urged the ratification of the Constitution, and he later served as Washington's secretary of the treasury. Hamilton's father-in-law, Philip Schuyler, lost his New York senate seat to Aaron, who had gained the support of the Clinton and Livingston families, both enemies of Schuyler. Thus began a hostility between Hamilton and Aaron that eventually would end in tragedy.

My son lost the 1800 presidential election to Thomas Jefferson by a whisker, largely due to the machinations of Hamilton, and so Aaron became vice president of the United States. When his term was almost over, he ran for governor of New York. Hamilton publicly campaigned against him, and his opposition tactics prevented my son from winning the seat he desired.

Furious over remarks that Hamilton allegedly made during the campaign, Aaron demanded a duel; Alexander reluctantly agreed. When the day came, they met at a dueling ground in Weehawken, New Jersey. Hamilton missed, but my son shot straight and true, fatally wounding his political rival.

Not long after the duel, Aaron became involved in a plot to create a new republic from territory west of the Appalachian Mountains, with a capital at New Orleans. He was arrested and tried for treason in 1807 but was acquitted due to lack of evidence. Following this escapade, Aaron went abroad in 1808. He returned to New York City in 1812 and resumed the practice of law, spending the rest of his days in pursuit of women and pleasure. My only son died in Port Richmond, Staten Island, New York, on September 14, 1836, and was interred beside me in the Princeton Cemetery.

I heard another squeal and a woman's voice said, "Tommy! Not in public." I sighed. Aaron was back, this time lurking near Nassau Hall. He had a strange look on his face—one of tenderness combined with desire. I drifted over to see what he was up to. Standing nearby was a small group of students; Aaron's eyes were fixed on a young woman who was talking animatedly among them.

"That one won't easily succumb to your wiles," I told him. "She looks like a woman of spirit and fire."

"She reminds me of my wife," Aaron said. There was a faraway note in his voice that I seldom heard.

Theodosia Prevost was Aaron's beloved first wife. She was the widow of a British officer and the mother of five children when Aaron met her. According to reports, Theodosia was a rather plain woman who possessed a highly educated, razor-sharp mind that transfixed Aaron, who previously had been well known for his pursuit of beautiful ladies. Stunned and very much in love, Aaron married the widow in 1782, and Theodosia gave birth to four more children, only one of whom survived. Little Theodosia was the light of Aaron's life after her mother and namesake died in 1794.

I tried to pursue the matter, but Aaron was so taken with the girl that he paid me no heed. Finally, I left him to his solitary reverie and went on my way.

I watched with amusement as Aaron ceased his shenanigans among the college girls and took to following his dead wife's look-alike around campus. I caught a glimpse then of the very great love Aaron still had for his first wife, and in that moment I was proud of my son. But, as I tried to point out to him, this girl was not Theodosia. If he persisted in following her about, sooner or later the spirited lass would take offense. He did not listen.

Two weeks after he first saw the girl, Aaron found her studying alone in a classroom, her books scattered all over the desk. She was standing at the blackboard, studying a mathematical equation, when he materialized. Aaron walked up to her, embraced her from behind, and whispered in her ear: "Come to me, my proud beauty."

The girl stiffened and glanced down at the semitransparent arms embracing her. Then she lashed out with her elbow, catching Aaron in the solar plexus. He gasped and released his grip. The girl whirled around to face him.

"Just who do you think you are?" she cried, slapping him first on one check and then on the other. Aaron had forgotten to dematerialize, so the slaps whipped his head back and forth sharply. The girl stalked to the door, threw it open, and then turned to confront the startled ghost. "I am not that kind of girl," she told him firmly and walked out of the room, leaving a stunned Aaron alone with her books.

I materialized at the back of the room, laughing so hard that I couldn't speak. I just pointed repeatedly at my son, then at the door where the student had departed, and then back at Aaron. He glared at me, rubbing his cheek, but finally he laughed, too.

"She definitely resembles Theodosia," he said, "in more ways than one."

"You'd better leave her alone from now on," I replied when I could draw enough breath.

"I suppose you are right," Aaron conceded ruefully.

"And if I were you, I'd get out of here before she returns for her books," I added for good measure.

Aaron looked alarmed at the thought. He vanished at once, and that was the last I saw of him that day. The next morning, I heard some squealing along the path where Aaron always lurks, and I smiled to myself. It seemed that he had given up his obsession and was back to his old tricks.

Just then, Aaron materialized in the room beside me and flopped down dramatically in a chair. He looked pale.

"What's wrong?" I asked.

"I almost ran into her!" he exclaimed. "She was coming down the walkway while I was . . . um . . . admiring the girls outside. When she heard them squealing, a purposeful look came over her face and she raised her notebook. She looked right over to where I was standing and started walking toward me. I wasn't even visible!" He mopped his forehead. "I think I am going to have to lay low for a while, perhaps until she graduates."

"That might be a very good idea," I said, hiding a grin.

Rising to his feet, my son made a formal bow and then disappeared. When he was gone, I laughed out loud. Then I went back to my studies, happy that I would be left in peace at my beloved university. At least for the moment.

15

Shades of Death

The darn kids were always stealing the road signs. Actually, it was not just the kids; some adults also thought it was cool to have a huge green and white sign that said SHADES OF DEATH ROAD. So whenever I had a moment, I would hike up to the intersection closest to my house and coat the pole with goose grease, to make climbing it difficult if not downright impossible. I considered it my little contribution to the neighborhood.

A car pulled up beside me in the dusk of a beautiful summer night, and a voice called, "Hey mister, do you know where Shades of Death Road is?" I calmly placed a little more goose grease on the pole, looked up at the street sign, and said, "You're on it, son."

From inside the car I heard chuckles of relief. "I told you we weren't lost," the lad's girlfriend said from the passenger side. The boy thanked me and drove off down the road, looking for adventure. Sometimes the silly young ones found it, sometimes they didn't.

Having finished with the grease, I carefully wiped the paintbrush and put everything away in my backpack. Shouldering it, I started walking down the beautiful woodland road on which I made my home. It was a shady spot, which is why it originally was called Shades Road. But it was also off the beaten track, narrow, and windy. Both wildcats and robbers had found it a convenient place to attack and kill travelers. In the late 1700s, many members of the local Lenape tribe contracted malaria carried by mosquitoes from a nearby swamp and began dying off. The road gained such a gloomy reputation that the name was changed to Shades of Death Road.

For those with the eyes to see, the spirits of the Lenape still linger here, rising with the fog over Ghost Lake and retreating only with the return of day. Most people drive right through the ghosts without seeing them. Of course, people are usually looking for more dramatic specters, like the evil spirit of the woman who murdered and decapitated her husband, burying his head on one side of the road and his body on the other. Or the ghost who stomps around the lake grounds and then retreats to an abandoned cabin, leaving footsteps in the mud or the snow, depending on the season. One girl I won't name claimed to have been chased down the road by a single glowing light that was as tall as a truck's headlights, though there was no truck behind her. The stories are numerous, and many of them are false. But not all.

I have a few drops of Lenape blood in me, and I am one of the few who can see the shades of my brothers rising with the fog. This particular night seemed like a good one for a sighting, which was part of the reason I chose to walk all the way to the intersection with my goose grease at dusk. Great pillars of fog were rising off Ghost Lake. Around me, dusk had deepened into night, but I knew the way well and walked without a flashlight. I didn't need one; the glow from the ghosts lit my way.

I watched a shining canoe move across the water, paddled by two Lenape intent on reaching their destination, wherever that was. They passed right through a group of men dancing and singing around a fire. I stopped to observe the dancers, knowing that when they finished a storyteller would appear and speak the age-old tales of our people. Right on cue, a venerable old man stood up among the crowd. Leaning gravely upon a stick for support, he began the creation story with "*Kunakwat, lowat, nuchink*," meaning "Long, long ago, in the beginning." The old man spoke of how there was nothing at all in the beginning except endless space in which the Creator dwelt. Then the Creator had a vision of the sun and the moon and the stars and the Earth. He dreamed that on Earth there were mountains and valleys and trees; land and sea; creatures that crawled and walked, slept and ate, loved, hated, lived, and died. He touched the wind, feeling all the emotions of those to come. Then the Creator's vision faded, and he determined to make his dream become reality.

Slowly I moved on, watching Lenape women cooking over small fires that flickered within the fog, and nodding to a few Lenape hunters who silently passed me on the road. From the middle of the lake, I saw a huge turtle emerge with some mud upon the back of its shell. It was Taxkwâx, the turtle that carried new Earth on its back after old Earth was drowned in a great flood. Nanapush, the Strong Pure One, the Grandfather of Beings and Men, had sent several animals to old Earth to retrieve some mud from which to make the new. Little Muskrat was the only creature to survive the trip. Nanapush placed the mud Little Muskrat had retrieved from the depths onto the back of Taxkwâx, who swam through the floodwaters while a great

SHADES OF DEATH

island grew and grew above him. This was new Earth, called Turtle Island. As a reward for his help, Taxkwâx became the messenger of thoughts and feelings between different beings.

I was nearly home when I heard a beautiful song coming from the trees. Looking into the branches overhead, I saw a glowing bird with bright feathers of many colors. I recognized him at once: It was Rainbow Crow, who had brought fire down from heaven to Earth to warm its inhabitants after the coming of the cold. As he carried the hot flame in his beak, he was burned black, his lovely voice choked so that he could only caw from that moment forward. Because his bravery saved the life of the creatures of Earth, he is honored by all animals and hunters. And the Creator himself placed a hint of a rainbow within Crow's shiny black feathers, as a reminder of the great sacrifice he made.

I turned into my driveway and saw the familiar figures of a Lenape father and son standing before their round wigwam, discussing something seriously. I nodded to them as I walked slowly past, and they nodded back. Moments later the front light snapped on and my wife opened the door. She was not blessed with the spirit sight, and she urged me to come in out of the darkness and the damp night air. With a small sigh, I left the shades of death in the past and came back to the present.

As I followed my wife into the house, I heard the drumbeat start again and knew that the ancient one's story had finished and the dancing had begun once more, deep inside the pillars of fog over Ghost Lake.

16

The Major General

JOCKEY HOLLOW, MORRISTOWN NATIONAL HISTORIC PARK

Davey raced down the path toward the visitor center, excited by our impromptu visit to Jockey Hollow on this lovely Saturday afternoon in late spring. My sister and I strolled behind, enjoying his antics but feeling no need to join in. It was a lazy kind of day, and there was no rush to be anywhere. My favorite kind of day.

Davey held the visitor center door open for us like a gentleman, only the jiggling of his leg betraying his desire for us to *hurry up already*. Then he was off into the gift shop to look at books and toys while my sister and I planned our visit with the woman staffing the desk.

I'd always associated Jockey Hollow with winter—the park was a favorite childhood sledding destination—and this was oddly appropriate since it had been the winter encampment for George Washington's Continental Army in 1779–80. After the defeat of the British at Princeton and Trenton, General Washington needed to find a place to winter his soldiers. He chose Morristown because it was close to New York City but was protected from attack by the Watchung Mountains to the east and the Ramapo Mountains to the north. Few roads pierced this section of New Jersey, and those were easily defended. The elevation also allowed the Americans to watch over the British lines to the east.

The soldiers' encampment at Jockey Hollow was considered favorable because the land had abundant forests, which allowed the men to build a log-house city precisely laid out in rows of eight. Folks reckon the soldiers cut down more than 600 acres of forest to build more than 1,000 log huts. These rough fourteen-by-fifteen-foot cabins, which slept twelve men apiece, were pretty much the only thing that stood between the ragged army and freezing to death that harsh winter.

The winter of 1779–80 was the coldest on record at the time. There was already a foot of snow on the ground when the soldiers—worn-out from six years of war—arrived in Jockey Hollow, and they recorded seven separate blizzards in December alone. Some storms produced six feet of snow in one go and were so blinding that the soldiers could not venture outside for fear of freezing to death a few feet from their door.

The roads became impassable to supply wagons and to dispatch riders. Food was so scarce that some soldiers ate their own boots or gnawed on the bark from trees to alleviate their hunger. Illnesses were frequent and desertions were commonplace. At one point conditions grew so bad that the ink inside pens froze even when the writer huddled close to the fire, and the roads were elevated by snow nearly twelve feet above their ordinary level.

The only communications came from soldiers on snowshoes, which caused frustrating delays in intelligence on enemy movements. It grew so cold that New York Harbor froze over and the British gained an advantage over the Continental Army. They used the iced-in harbor and rivers as roads and began supplying their troops via ox-drawn sleighs. When they began moving their heavy artillery, Washington was forced to send out his own troops to discourage the British army and keep them safely contained within New York City.

Thankfully, in spite of all the hardship and suffering, there was still a Continental Army left when spring finally arrived. And that army went on to win several decisive battles and gain America its independence from Great Britain.

After gathering information at the visitor center, we decided to visit the Wick House, which was within easy walking distance. According to the literature provided by the National Park Service, Henry Wick was a wealthy Morristown resident who owned the 1,400-acre farm on which the log-house city was constructed. Major General Arthur St. Clair, who was the commander of 2,000 soldiers from Pennsylvania, was quartered in Henry Wick's house during the Jockey Hollow encampment.

Karen, Davey, and I meandered through a lovely green woodland full of birdsong and rustling leaves. Soon we spied a small Cape Cod–style house with a fenced-in garden beside it. As we followed the garden fence toward the house, my sister slowed down. Karen had told me on numerous occasions that the land all around Jockey Hollow was haunted. A quick glance at her face indicated that she sensed something about the house ahead of us. I took a breath and reached out with my own sixth sense, which instantly confirmed that the house was haunted. Davey was trotting eagerly toward the building, which was furnished to portray its use as a Revolutionary War general's headquarters.

"Hurry!" he cried, bouncing on his toes. I glanced at the dark windows of the house. The ghostly chill was still there, but I didn't see anything obvious.

"Do you want to go in?" I asked my sister, sotto voce.

"I think we have to," she said, nodding at her son. Yes, she was right. It wasn't fair to deprive Davey of a treat, not to mention some good old-fashioned historical knowledge, just because a house was (probably) haunted.

The back door was open and led into the large kitchen area. Davey marched inside and a man in Colonial costume greeted him. I stepped over the threshold just behind my sister. The sense of another unseen presence was stronger inside the building. It wasn't a scary feeling so much as an uneasy pressure along my skin. There was more here than met the eye.

And what met the eye was quite interesting. The room was furnished with a large kitchen table, a fireplace with pots and cooking utensils, candles in various stages of use, drying herbs hanging from the ceiling, and much more. As the Colonial-garbed volunteer discussed the history of Wick House with my wide-eyed nephew, my sister looked around with a funny expression on her face, lips pressed together, as she took in our invisible company.

As Davey and the man discussed what it was like to live in Revolutionary War times, I stepped into the next room and stopped abruptly with a small gasp. A figure stood in an open side door on my left, which led to the guest bedroom. I could sense the phantom so clearly that it was almost as if I could see him. Yet he remained invisible.

The ghost bowed and I heard his name in my head as if he'd spoken aloud: "Arthur St. Clair, at your service." It was the Major General himself. Then St. Clair walked past me and went to stand beside the front window of the house. His back to the glass, he watched with interest as I nervously looked over the exhibit.

I heard footsteps behind me and turned in time to see my sister enter the room. Her eyes flew instantly to the window where the Major General stood. I wondered what she saw there but didn't want to ask in case we were overheard by the volunteer in the kitchen. I think the Major General bowed to her, too.

Davey came trotting into the room after us and peered excitedly at the sample soldier's uniform, the small bed in the guest room, and the other items on display. His bright chatter made the ghost smile.

I led the way into the parlor on the far side of the house, which was outfitted with a desk and a few other period pieces. The Major General followed us into the room. As he passed me, a series of pictures appeared in my head: ragged soldiers standing at attention as they gave their reports; snow blasting through the front door before it was properly shut; St. Clair rubbing his forehead wearily; a woman bending over a boiling pot while the mouth-watering scent of fresh bread filled the room.

The room temperature dropped suddenly, as if my vision of the winter storm had frozen the air around us. I shivered, still smelling fresh bread mingled with the crisp scent of snow. The chill made my nostrils ache.

"It's cold in here," Davey said. "I'm going back to the kitchen." He trotted briskly away to ask more questions of the Colonial-garbed volunteer.

"Gee, I wonder why it's so cold in here?" his mother murmured ironically, giving me a very pointed look as she followed her son. She ignored the ghost standing by the desk.

I glanced over at the Major General, who smiled at me.

"Don't forget to ask about the horse," he said. Then he strode smartly across the house, retreating to his small bedroom to await the next crop of visitors.

The horse? *What horse?* I wondered. There was only one way to find out.

When I reached the kitchen, I asked the volunteer: "Someone told me to ask about a horse when I visited Jockey Hollow. Do you know the story?" I placed a slight emphasis on the word *someone*, and my sister looked up sharply from a copper pot she was inspecting by the fireplace.

"You must mean the story of Tempe Wick," the volunteer said delightedly.

A year after the Jockey Hollow encampment, a Pennsylvania brigade was stationed in the vicinity of Morristown. Angry because their wages were long overdue, some of the soldiers mutinied against their superiors. The soldiers caused havoc throughout the countryside, stealing from the local residents and commandeering any horses they found.

It was a very bad time to venture away from home, but Tempe Wick had no choice. Her mother was very ill and needed immediate medical attention. Praying she would not encounter the mutineers, Tempe saddled her horse and rode to the doctor's house, where she left a message begging him to come tend her sick mother. On the way home, three soldiers stepped out of the woods to confront Tempe on the road. One of the men grabbed the bridle of her horse and demanded that she give them her mount. Displaying fear (which she no doubt felt), Tempe pretended to give in to the soldier's demands and requested assistance in dismounting. When the soldier stepped to her side to help her down, Tempe whipped her horse and galloped for home.

THE MAJOR GENERAL

Knowing the mutineers would follow her, Tempe led the horse right inside her family's house and hid him in the guest bedroom. She tied the horse to the wall, closed the shutters so no one could see inside, and placed a featherbed under his hooves to muffle any movements he made. When the soldiers arrived, they searched the property, the woods, and all the outbuildings but no one looked inside the house, so they never found the horse. Some folks claim Tempe Wick kept the horse quartered inside until the mutineers marched south to Princeton on New Year's Day.

"Great story!" I exclaimed when the volunteer finished.

Karen was hovering near the door. I knew she wanted to get away from the haunted house, so I thanked the volunteer and we went outside to look at the well and explore the herb garden, which was coming along nicely in the warm spring weather.

"Did you see him?" I asked casually as Davey raced along the rows of plants.

"Yes," Karen replied. "It was the Major General that the man in the kitchen was talking about."

"Arthur St. Clair," I said.

At that moment Davey shouted for his mother, wanting her to look at some flowers growing on the far side of the garden. As Karen followed my nephew deeper into the scented herbs, I glanced toward the window of the haunted guest bedroom. I had a sudden thought: If people could return as ghosts, did that mean horses could, too? And if that were the case, was the ghostly Major General sharing his small bedroom with a horse? The thought made me chuckle.

I lifted my hand and waved to the ghost of Wick House (and possibly to the horse). Then I raced after my sister and her son.

17

Guardian of the Great Swamp

MORRIS COUNTY

When the grandkids said they wanted to take a Sunday afternoon walk around the trails at the Great Swamp, I tried to palm the task off on my wife. It wasn't because I didn't like hanging out with the grandkids. Quite the opposite. It was the Great Swamp that bothered me. I hadn't been there since . . . well, since the troubles happened back when I was a young husband and an employee of the Port Authority. And that was a long time ago. Not going to the Great Swamp was a habit now, and a hard one to break. But my wife was up to her elbows in preparations for a vast Sunday dinner and could not be interrupted for a walk. So it was up to me.

I piled into the car with three giggling grandkids. A huge bag of potato chips was passed back and forth over the front seat as we drove to the Great Swamp. While the kids chattered like magpies and sang songs with their favorite CD, I thought about the last time I'd visited the Great Swamp.

Back in 1959 the Port Authority was looking for a place to put a new regional airport. The Great Swamp was proposed as a potential site, so I was sent to look it over. In those days the Great Swamp was filled with trees, muddy ponds, grasslands, and a great variety of wildlife. And about a million mosquitoes. Blast it, I was a target as soon as I stepped out of the car and got bitten to death inspecting the place.

I had to admit the Great Swamp was beautiful. Deer were plentiful, as well as muskrats, fish, turtles, frogs, and birds of every shape and size. In a way, it was a shame to destroy such a lovely spot. But we really needed a regional airport, and this location seemed to fit the requirements.

As I marched through the bog, I kept twitching as if unseen eyes were watching me. The deeper I went into the swamp, the colder I got—even though it was a balmy sixty degrees that day—and I seemed to be at the center of a strange silence. It was creepy. The sun was shining and I could hear birds chirping and frogs croaking and the wind rustling the leaves overhead, but the noises were muffled as if someone had put a huge blanket over my ears. I became so alarmed that I turned back and stumbled through woods, swamp, and overgrown meadow until I reached the road where I'd parked the car.

By the time I got back to the road, I was sure I was being followed, though I never caught a glimpse of the person doing the following. I hightailed it out of there on the double and kept checking my rearview mirror until I was safe on the highway. Shaken, I gave my report to my supervisor and went home early, my head pounding with stress.

That night, I had the first of a series of dreams. In my dream, a Native warrior was walking through the Great Swamp, using the same deer path I'd been following that morning. In his prime, the man was tall and bare-chested, wearing only deerskin pants and moccasins on his feet. A few muskrat pelts were tossed casually over his shoulder, and he carried a bow and quiver full of arrows. A menacing war club hung at his side. The warrior looked up and saw me. At once he frowned, eyes narrow with anger, and I felt a chill pass over me. I sensed that the warrior was the guardian of the place called the Great Swamp. He knew why I came to inspect the land, and he did not approve.

Not long after my inspection, the Port Authority of New York announced their proposal for a new state-of-the-art jetport. The airport would encompass 10,000 acres of land in southeastern Morris County, 4,000 of which comprised the Great Swamp. Immediately conservationists were up in arms, and a nonprofit was formed to oppose the airport. They assembled a large pool of volunteers and started collecting money, circulating petitions, and disseminating information.

As the public relations departments from both sides of the debate fought it out in the public arena, I fought it out in my head. At least once a week, I encountered the guardian of the Great Swamp in my dreams. Usually I was walking along a trail through the swamp, heading toward a pretty pond on the far side of a copse of trees. Somewhere along the path, the guardian would appear and walk along beside me. At first, he seemed sorrowful. But as the disagreement between the Port Authority and the conservationists escalated, the guardian grew angry.

When the fight dragged into a second year, the guardian began menacing me in my dreams. He would appear out of nowhere, club raised for a killing blow, and I would flee in terror for my life. Sometimes I escaped to the road and drove off in my car, with his massive figure chasing behind me. Sometimes I ran and ran through the woods, hopelessly lost, hearing pounding footsteps getting closer to me. Once, I veered off the path and accidentally plunged into an unseen waterhole. My clothes and shoes kept dragging me under the surface, and I woke gasping in panic just before I drowned.

After that last dream, my wife dragged me to the doctor's office to see if something could be done about the nightmares. But nothing helped. The only way to appease the guardian was to cancel the jetport project, and I was not responsible for making that decision. Finally the Port Authority gave in to local pressure. After two years of fighting, the proposed Morris County jetport project was history.

The last dream I had of the guardian of the Great Swamp was on Christmas Eve 1961. We were walking side by side along the deer path through the woods, our feet tromping through a couple of inches of new-fallen snow. The warrior wore a buckskin shirt and a deer hide wrapped around him for warmth. I felt cowed and sheepish, but he was smiling and triumphant. We stopped at the edge of a pond and watched the snow falling on a pair of ducks that were huddled sleepily by a small log. It was a very beautiful scene, and I was glad that the jetport proposal had failed. Then I awoke, and knew this was the last time the guardian of the Great Swamp would visit my dreams.

Soon afterward, the nonprofit organization turned its attention toward permanently preserving the Great Swamp from development. The Great Swamp Committee raised a few million dollars and purchased several thousand acres of the swamp to donate to the Department of the Interior for a national wildlife refuge. I was pleased when I read about this conservation effort in the local paper, but I felt guilty over my role in the jetport debate and was still afraid of the guardian of the Great Swamp, in spite of the peace I felt between us in my last dream. So I decided I would leave the Great Swamp for others to enjoy and would use other, less memory-fraught areas to pursue outdoor activities in the future.

Now, as I drove down the familiar road leading to the Great Swamp, all the memories and the fears from that two-year struggle came flooding back. As I pulled onto the dirt-and-gravel road leading to the parking area, my hands were shaking on the steering wheel. In my mind, I felt the dark waters of the swamp closing over my head as they'd done in my nightmare. I pictured my terrible struggle to reach the surface, to take a breath and not drown.

The grandkids piled out of the car, laughing and calling. Their smiles dispelled some of my apprehension. The Great Swamp was a national wildlife refuge now. The guardian was appeased. There was no need to fear.

We clustered around the posted map, and then the grandkids went laughing and skipping along the boardwalk toward the first of the wildlife observation blinds, pausing to lean over the railings to look for fish and frogs. Huge dragonflies fluttered among the lily pads. Birds whistled and chirped. A large turtle popped its head out of the water and blinked at me. I blinked back.

When they finished gazing out every window of the wildlife observation blind overlooking pond and meadow, I proposed hiking the trail to a second observation blind about a half-mile distant. (I needed to do something to get out all that energy before dinner!) The kids raced ahead, pausing at a small bridge to exclaim over a muskrat before plunging into the woods beyond. As I followed them across the bridge, the sounds around me muted suddenly and the air grew ice cold. When I stepped onto the far bank of the stream, I felt as if I had stepped into the setting of my long-ago nightmares. The woods looked exactly like the forest I'd walked so many times in my dreams. I stopped, heart pounding, wanting to turn back. But my grandkids were ahead of me in those woods, and it was my duty to protect them from harm. I stepped onto the path and hurried after those precious not-so-little kids.

As I walked, I realized that there was someone walking beside me. I could not see him, but I knew he was there, matching me step for step. Just ahead, the grandkids had climbed onto a fallen log. They waved enthusiastically at me from their perch. I waved back and wondered if they could see my invisible companion. Apparently not. The kids jumped off the log and raced toward the observation blind just ahead. I followed them, feeling dizzy. I recognized this place, though I'd never been here before. It was the location I'd visited in my final dream of the guardian. It was the place where I stood in that dream, watching the early snow falling on two sleeping ducks.

When I reached the blind, the grandkids excitedly pointed to a blue heron wading in the water. We also saw a few Canada geese and a plethora of ducks. Then the kids retreated back along the hiking trail, hoping to see the muskrat again when they reached the stream.

I paused for a final look at the pond, rubbing goose bumps from my arms. When I turned around, I saw a Native American man sitting on a log a few feet from the blind. He was dark-haired and bare-chested, wearing only buckskin pants and soft moccasins on his feet. The war club was nowhere to be seen, but he still had a muskrat pelt over one shoulder. We gazed at one another for a timeless moment. Then I bowed to the guardian of the Great Swamp. He rose, gave me an acknowledging nod,

GUARDIAN OF THE GREAT SWAMP

and walked away. His body grew dimmer with each step until he vanished into thin air. I exhaled sharply, both frightened and relieved by the encounter. Apparently, I had been forgiven for that long-ago struggle.

I heard my grandkids calling excitedly and trotted down the path to join them by the stream. They'd spotted a giant bullfrog and wanted me to take a picture with my cell phone so they could show it to Grandma. After posing for a few more pictures—including one with the obliging muskrat—we hurried back to the car. Grandma's Sunday feast awaited us upon our return.

As I pulled out of the parking area, I glanced in my rearview mirror and saw a tall figure standing waist-deep in the wild grasses and flowers of the meadow. He raised a hand in greeting and farewell, then vanished in the blink of an eye. I smiled and turned right onto the road leading home.

18

The Ghost of Pearl White

JERSEY CITY

When I was a kid, my grandparents bought an old boardinghouse in Jersey City. It had once housed actresses working for a big silent film studio located directly across the street, but the film studio was long gone, and now the boardinghouse was unused. My grandparents converted it into a three-family home. They moved into the bottom floor, offered my parents the second floor, and rented out the third. It worked out pretty well for everyone. There was extra income for my grandparents; privacy for our family, with quick access to Grandma when it was wanted or needed; and a quiet couple on the third floor who provided additional income for my grandparents with no hassles.

Actually, the couple upstairs was a little too quiet. It was odd. No one's life could be that serene.

I was not sure how the idea got started in my small head—maybe I overheard my parents talking—but I soon got the notion that the wife in the upstairs apartment was a recluse. Occasionally my parents or grandparents would encounter the husband on his way to or from work, and he always chatted with the family for about ten minutes on the day he delivered the rent check. But the wife never appeared at all.

My parents sometimes speculated about this strange woman they never saw, but I didn't pay attention to their conversations. I was more concerned with dolls and school friends and playing in the sandbox in our backyard than with reclusive adults, so I ignored the whole situation.

Now, bedtime for me at the new house was 8:00 p.m. sharp. My bedroom was opposite the main staircase, and I could see it clearly when lying tucked up in my bed for the night. One evening about a month after we moved in, a strange lady wearing a gorgeous, fancy yellow dress strolled past my room at 8:15 and walked up the third-floor staircase.

I sat up in bed, mouth open in surprise. Who was she, and where had she come from? I shivered, for the air was suddenly cold in my bedroom. I was a little frightened by this strange person strolling calmly through my new house as if she owned it. I was about to yell for my mother when I realized who the woman must be. She was obviously the reclusive wife of our third-floor neighbor. I relaxed at once and lay back against the pillow.

She sure was a pretty lady, I thought as I drifted toward sleep. *And that dress was to die for!*

A couple of nights later, the lady strolled past my door again at 8:15 on the dot. This time she wore a pink dress with elaborate lace and carried a fan. I sat up and watched her with interest, rubbing my arms against the sudden chill in my room as she walked up the staircase and disappeared from view. I wanted my mother to make me a dress like that. I wondered if the reclusive third-floor lady could tell my mother the store where she had bought it. I snuggled under my covers with a smile. Maybe the store sold dresses like that in my size.

After that I saw the lady almost every night. She strolled past my door and walked up the third-floor staircase until she disappeared from sight. I loved the lady's clothes. Often she wore the yellow dress in which I'd first seen her. But sometimes her dress was blue or pink or white, with lovely lace or embroidery. *She must work in a very fancy store,* I thought. My mother never wore such long, fancy dresses, and she never wore her hair up with combs and jewels.

One night, about a year after we moved into the old boardinghouse, I was awakened from a deep sleep by a cold breeze that flapped the curtains on the window and rattled the coloring books on my desk. I blinked sleepily and saw a figure walk through my bedroom door. It was the lady from the third floor again. She was wearing the fancy pink dress with the fan, and her hair was pulled back with two lovely pearl-white combs. The woman walked over to my closet and went through the partially opened door. I blinked in surprise, for it seemed almost as if her body had gone through the wood of the door itself, rather than through the small opening between the door and the frame. But that was silly. No one could walk through wood! And why had she gone into my closet?

The cold wind ceased as abruptly as it began, and my sleep-fogged brain refused to wrestle with the mystery. I'd seen the lady every day for more than a year, and she'd never bothered me before. If she wanted to spend the night in my closet, so be it. As sleep claimed me, I decided that there must be a secret staircase in my closet that led to the third floor.

When I woke in the morning, I jumped out of bed and went into my closet. Sure enough, the lady wasn't there. I started tapping the walls and the ceiling, trying to discover the key to the secret door, but it eluded me. I'd have to ask the lady the next time she went upstairs at 8:15. Of course, I completely forgot about the secret door in the closet by bedtime, too caught up in my childhood dramas to remember the strange event of the previous night.

A few weeks later, my grandparents sold the old boardinghouse to my aunt and we moved into a nice home in the suburbs. So I never solved the mystery of the secret door in the closet.

About a month after the move, my aunt came stomping into our suburban house in a rage as I sat at the kitchen table, eating my after-school snack.

"I cannot believe you sold me a haunted house," my aunt said to my grandpa.

"What do you mean haunted?" Grandpa asked.

My aunt explained. Loudly. And in great detail. She ranted about the ghostly woman who walked up the third-floor staircase every night at 8:15 p.m. on the dot. And the previous night, the ghost had walked right into my aunt's room—my former bedroom—and had floated past her bed and right through the closet door.

I stared at my aunt, pop-eyed in amazement. The lady with the beautiful dresses had been a *ghost*? I could hardly believe it. I shivered a little, remembering the strange breeze that had fluttered the curtains of my room the night the lady walked into my closet. Then again, maybe I *could* believe it.

"You're crazy, Loretta. You must have been dreaming," my father said.

My grandfather shook his head sadly as he contemplated his poor, addled daughter and added, "Daughter, there is no such thing as a ghost."

THE GHOST OF PEARL WHITE

Realizing I had to defend my beleaguered aunt, I told my parents and grandparents about my own ghostly sightings. In the end they had to believe it, because both my aunt and I had seen the ghost many times.

A look through old photographs of female stars from the silent film era identified the ghost as that of Pearl White. Further research revealed that my closet had been the dressing room for some of the actresses. So that explained why the ghost had sometimes walked into my closet. (To own the truth, I was a bit disappointed that there was no secret staircase.)

To this day, I still have no idea why the ghost of Pearl White walks the halls of her old boardinghouse. Perhaps it is to remind herself of a happy period in her life? All I know for sure is that Pearl White is the best-dressed ghost in Jersey City! I'm still envious of her beautiful gowns.

19

Ring around the Rosie

HOWELL

"Ring around the rosie, a pocket full of posies . . ."

I hear the voices chanting in the woods and look up from my lonely sandbox, enchanted by the sound. There are little girls and boys playing games in the forest behind my house. Someone to play with at last!

When we lived in an apartment in the city, there were lots of children that I could play with. But now we live in a brand-new house outside the city, and there are only grown-up neighbors on our block. There is no one to play with in my new home. I feel lonely all the time. So the sound of singing, laughing children is very welcome to me. I jump up and race into the woods, shouting, "Hello! Hello!" But no one answers me.

I hear the other children giggling just over the ridge and run up the hill as fast as I can. I get to the top in record time, but no one is there. Around me, the woods feel empty. I turn around, kicking dispiritedly at the autumn leaves underfoot, and wander down the hill to my backyard and the sad little toys in my lonely sandbox.

While I eat dinner with Mama and Papa, I hear the children singing from the woods behind my house: "Ring around the

rosie, a pocket full of posies. Ashes, ashes, we all fall down!"
There is a dramatic thudding sound as several bodies tumble to
the ground, and then giggles. I drop my chicken leg onto my
plate and run to the window to look outside. All I see are trees.
No children.

"Come back to the table, Sarah, and finish your dinner,"
Mama scolds.

"But I want to play with the children in the woods," I
protest.

"What children in the woods?" Papa asks with interest.

"The ones who were singing just now," I say as I climb back
into my chair, which is nearly too tall for me, and pick up my
fried chicken with greasy fingers.

"No one was singing just now," Papa says, piling mashed
potatoes onto his plate. "What an imagination the child has,"
he adds, grinning at Mama before putting a big spoonful of
potatoes on my plate.

It is too dark to play outside when we finish supper, so I
must wait until morning to look for the singing children.

I roam alone in the woods the next morning, listening for
the sound of laughing voices. A new family must have moved
into our neighborhood, I decide. A big family with many
children. Their children are very shy. I hear them giggle and
whisper words that I cannot make out. I run toward the sound,
but they are too quick for me. It is like a game of hide-and-seek.
"Ollie ollie oxen free!" I shout, jumping out from behind a big
tree. But no one is there.

I hear the children laughing at me from the far side of the
ridge, where the ground drops suddenly into a steep ravine. I
am not allowed to play up there. Papa says it is too dangerous.

I cannot follow the children up that hill. I cannot break my promise to Papa. Sadly, I trudge away, going back to my lonely yard to play on the tire swing Papa tied to a tall tree.

At lunch I tell my mother about the game of hide-and-seek that the children are playing with me, but I know she doesn't believe me. She ruffles my hair and chuckles about my bright imagination. I find it odd that she cannot hear the children. They sing so loud: "Ring around the rosie, a pocket full of posies."

I ask Papa about the children when he gets home from work. He can't hear them either. He calls them my imaginary friends and says I will grow up to be a writer.

In the morning I wake to the sound of children's voices calling to me through the window. "Little girl, come and play," they sing over and over in my ears. The children sound like so much fun that I run outside as fast as I can to try to catch them. I plunge into the woods, calling back to the children, but no one answers. So I stand still as a mouse, trying to hear where they are hiding. Then I hear Mama calling from the house, "Sarah! Time for breakfast." As I hurry home, I hear giggles and the children start to sing: "Ring around the rosie, a pocket full of posies." Oh, why are they so shy?

It starts to rain after breakfast, so I stay inside putting a puzzle together in the living room while Mama has coffee with a neighbor lady.

"I wouldn't live here for any amount of money," the neighbor lady says to Mama. "The woods behind the house are haunted."

"Haunted?" Mama says in the bright tone she uses when she doesn't believe what someone is saying.

"Yes, haunted," the neighbor lady confirms. "Back in Colonial times, a local family was fleeing from the British when a Revolutionary battle swung too close to their farm. Bullets flew everywhere, and cannons exploded all around. The father was wounded by a bullet, and the mother told her three children to flee into the woods while she followed with their injured father. The terrified children could barely see for all the smoke from the nearby cannons. They fled to the top of the ridge, and the youngest slipped and fell into the ravine. The middle child stumbled and rolled after him, but the hem of her skirt was caught by her elder brother at the very edge of the ravine. Then the cloth ripped, and the little girl tumbled to her death in the stream far below. Her elder brother, making a last desperate grab for his sister, fell too and smashed onto the rocks between his two dead siblings. People say that the children's ghosts still roam the forest behind this house. They are lonely and often call to living children, asking them to come play with them. But this is a death summons. Any child who answers their call is doomed to die in the ravine as they did, for living children cannot play with ghosts."

"Hush," Mama says fiercely, looking around to see if I'd overheard this gruesome tale. "You will scare my daughter."

"Good," the neighbor lady replies unrepentantly. "Maybe she will stay out of the woods. They are not safe for a young child."

"You are talking complete nonsense," Mama says sharply. "Let's speak about something else." And she asks my neighbor if anyone in the area plays bridge.

I think about the neighbor's story while I finish my puzzle. She means well, but she obviously doesn't know what she is talking about, I decide. The children in the woods are real people. They laugh and sing and dance. Ghosts don't laugh and sing. Ghosts are scary creatures. They would never play "Ring around the Rosie."

While I am eating my breakfast the next morning, I hear the children call to me from the woods. "Sarah, come out and play," they cry. They know my name! Now that we are introduced, they will have to let me play with them. I finish my breakfast so fast that the milk spills from my cereal bowl. Then I run outside with my blue smock still dripping wet.

"Where are you?" I call as I run into the woods. I hear them giggling. Their footsteps scamper first here, then there. I laugh aloud and follow them uphill and down. They are always just out of sight. Then they start singing somewhere near the top of the forbidden ridge, "Ring around the rosie, a pocket full of posies!" I race up the hill and careen down the far side. At last I see them! The children are right in front of me, dancing in a circle on the edge of the ridge. Their clothing looks a bit strange and their bodies flicker around the edges, but I am too busy running to notice.

Then my foot slips in the loose dirt and I slide down the hill on my bottom. I am going very fast, too fast. The ravine is directly in front of me, and I can see black cliffs with jagged outcroppings like sharp teeth. If I tumble over the edge, there is a steep drop of a hundred feet onto hard, sharp rocks in the water of the stream far below.

I scream and call to the children for help. They are still dancing in a circle, singing, "Ring around the rosie, a pocket full of posies." I don't think they can hear me. I am sliding faster and faster down the slope, banging painfully against rocks and

RING AROUND THE ROSIE

vainly trying to grab roots—anything to stop my fall. My heart pounds with fear, and I am sweating and cold by turns.

"Help me!" I scream as my body pitches off the edge of the cliff. For a moment, I hang in the air above the ravine like a floating feather. Ice-cold bands close around my chest as I realize that the children are dancing in a circle in midair, far above the rocky floor of the ravine. As I plummet through the middle of their game, their ice-cold bodies chill my skin. I scream and fall for a long, long time. For the rest of my too-short life. Above me, the children's voices are still singing, "Ring around the rosie."

20

Haunted Birthday

PEAPACK

The strangest thing happened to me last Friday. I say *strange* because *eerie* is an uncomfortable word. But what happened was truly eerie in the most uncomfortable way imaginable.

Friday was my sister's birthday, and for her birthday present she wanted to take a special Mansion in May tour in Peapack. The popular event, which uses a mansion to showcase the work of local interior and landscape designers, is a rare opportunity to take a sneak peek into one of the fabulous houses in the area. You have to grab tickets as soon as you can before they're sold out. If you miss the event, you'll have to wait for several years before that particular mansion comes up again in the rota.

The featured house this year just so happened to be the place where my sister saw a ghost many years ago, when she and her boyfriend were sneaking around the grounds of the then-derelict mansion at midnight. My sister was wild to see it in its newly restored state, and I was happy to oblige her. Her description of the ghost she'd seen standing in the window seemed fairly benign, so I figured it was safe to tour the mansion, especially as we were going on a sunny Friday afternoon and the mansion would be full of gawking tourists. Nothing spooky could possibly happen.

Cars were not allowed on the grounds, so we had to take the tour bus across town. As soon as we entered the grounds of the mansion, I felt nauseous. I was overwhelmed by a sense of malevolence so strong, I wanted to shout for the bus driver to stop and let me off. Good Lord! Whatever had happened here had left a strong residue, and more than one spirit haunted the place, if I was any judge.

My sister took one look at my face and grinned a little. "I told you this place was haunted," she said.

"You weren't kidding," I managed to gasp, and then fell silent, trying to quell the nausea and ward myself against the supernatural. Oddly, the feeling abated somewhat once we were past the gate and the first outbuildings. Or perhaps I grew used to it. By the time the bus paused beside the reflecting pool outside the entrance to the mansion, I felt almost normal.

As soon as we were out of the bus, my sister rushed me down the long drive and around to the terraces on the side of the mansion to show me where she'd stood when she saw the ghost in the second-floor window. I caught a glimpse of a huge crow crouched on the closest chimney. It made a grating sound I had never before heard from a corvine, and another crow answered from the far side of the house. For a moment it seemed as though they were saying "Evil! Evil!" I shuddered and looked away.

My sister pointed toward the window where, one night long ago, she had seen the ghostly figure of a woman. No woman was visible now, but I could sense a menacing presence lurking in the building. I shuddered. No wonder the crows were croaking "Evil!" The birds were right about that.

We walked all around the building, gazing at the views while my sister replicated the path she had taken on her earlier trip to the mansion. She pointed out the terrace where her former boyfriend heard a ghost following him within the house, rattling its keys. I shivered and suggested we start the formal house tour.

My sister and I entered through the front door of the house. Simultaneously we paused as our inherited sixth sense proclaimed a strong supernatural presence in the building. There was more than one ghost, I thought as a guide greeted us and gave us the standard beginning of the tour.

As we moved from newly decorated room to newly decorated room, my sister and I became fixated on finding the original features of the house: door frames, bookcases, the old elevator shaft. The haunting seemed tied somehow to these original objects.

When we entered the billiard room, my gaze was caught by the painting of an old man over the fireplace. I felt the temperature in the room drop as we stared at it. My arms broke out in goose bumps, and I asked the attendant about the picture. He was the original owner's grandfather, she told me. I knew the old man was important somehow. Either he or his son was connected to this room. My sister, wandering into the room a moment later, also stared at the picture with widened eyes. When we compared notes later, she told me she had received the same impression of significance that I had when viewing the portrait.

My sister beckoned me out into the little hall and asked me to look into the elevator shaft window. As I gazed inside, I was overwhelmed by a wave of coldness and malice so fierce that I staggered backward. My sister gave me her half-smile that said, "Told you! Haunted."

"Thanks a lot," I muttered back and followed her toward the central hallway, where an attendant told us to walk upstairs. I hung back with a gulp. Something hovered on the staircase. And the huge statue that loomed by the windows on the landing was very wrong. It should not have been chosen for a haunted house. The statue was encouraging the haunting. Yuck.

My sister was already partway up the staircase, so I followed her lead. The ghost she'd seen in the window haunted the second floor. And we were heading inexorably toward that haunted room as we continued the self-guided tour.

I entered a room that was made to look like a lounge and was immediately addressed by a ghostly man who was standing by the window overlooking the terrace. Clairaudience—a gift I'd inherited from my Pennsylvania Dutch great-grandfather—is an uneasy gift at best. It means that sometimes you can talk to spirits, and you can hear what they say to you. This man welcomed me to his home. He was the late owner—the son of the man in the portrait—and this was once his master bedroom. He was thrilled that someone could hear him and wanted me to stay, but I felt uncomfortable and soon left the room to its invisible occupant.

When we reached a small room done up in pink for a little girl, I grew nauseous again. Something bad had happened in this room. Beside me, my sister nearly burst into tears and could hardly breathe. We walked through the attached bathroom, which stood between the child's bedroom and the chamber where my sister had seen the ghost so many years ago. By this time, I had goose bumps all over. Something on this side of the house was not right, *not right!*

My sister waved me toward the haunted bedchamber, wanting me to go first. I tensed and then walked into the beautifully decorated bedroom, prepared for anything. To my surprise, it didn't feel much different from the other rooms in the house. It was haunted, yes, but at the moment, no more so than any of the others. My sister and I started photographing the room. As we did, the temperature dropped twenty degrees and something huge and swirling and angry began manifesting itself right over our heads. We ran, my sister in the lead with me right behind. My sister paused in the next chamber and I frantically pushed her onward. The ghost was following us, and for some reason it was really mad at my sister. If my sister stayed anywhere in the vicinity, everyone on this side of the house would soon be able to see the ghost—she was that close to manifesting in the physical realm. I pushed my sister through a third room, done over like a fancy lady's dressing room, and then out into the hallway.

"The ghost, she's tied to me. She won't let me go," my sister gasped.

"Do you want me to talk to her?" I asked.

"Yes, make her leave me alone!" my sister cried and fled into the next room.

I whirled on my heels, walked into the room where a docent was demonstrating his state-of-the-art equipment to some tourists, and silently demanded that the ghostly woman speak to me. She came instantly, angry but obedient to my summons. Around me, the temperature dropped like a stone through water. When I invoked my authority a second time, the air began to swirl and sparkle around me. My hair blew upward in the breeze created by the agitated spirit's presence. I hastily moved into the empty chamber next door before the other tourists noticed something supernatural was going on behind them.

Alone with the ghost, I demanded that she release my sister.

The phantom nearly howled with rage. *Your sister is a trespasser. She shouldn't be here!* The ghost was furious. *Anger! Rage!*

You will let her go, I told the ghost.

No, she replied sullenly.

We sparred verbally for a few tense minutes, both of us knowing who would win this fight. The ghost was acting like a sulky child. At last, she grudgingly released her hold on my sister. As soon as she did, the air in the room lightened.

Several tourists were making their way into the chamber where I was speaking with the ghost, so I pulled out my camera and pretended to be taking pictures as a disguise while I retraced my steps back through the dressing room and into the hall beyond. The ghost followed me, discontented and grumbling.

At that moment, my sister came jauntily into the hallway. "The ghost let me go," she said. "She's gone."

I glared at her. "She is not gone. She is right here with me. And if you don't go away right now, she is going to latch onto you again."

My sister turned pale and rushed into the dressing room, walking right through the ghost in the process. Thankfully, the phantom's attention was still fixed on me. She ignored my sister and we continued our silent dialogue. Finally, I convinced the ghost to return to her accustomed place by the window. Once she was gone, my sister and I were free to finish the tour in peace.

HAUNTED BIRTHDAY

I almost collapsed when we exited the house via the dining room, exhausted by the energy it took to release my sister from the ghost. I glared at her as we made our way toward the buses lining the front drive.

"Why do I visit these places with you?" I grumbled. "You always stir up the ghosts and then leave me to deal with them!"

"Because you love me?" she suggested

I just shook my head. "After this crazy trip, I think I deserve a steak dinner. Your treat," I said. "Let's go home."

PART TWO

Powers of Darkness and Light

21

On Washington Rock

The dream was so vivid that she didn't realize at first that it was a dream. The party was crowded, the guests cheerful, the food delicious. Then a rumor began to circulate among the guests. The Devil was coming to the party. The Devil was on his way.

Moments later a hush came over the crowd. Turning to locate its cause, she saw a tall, handsome blond man standing in the doorway, greeting his hostess. Around her the murmurs began again. It was the Devil. He had come.

Out of the corner of her eye, she saw the Devil making the rounds. He looked so ordinary that she found it hard to believe that he was, in fact, the Devil. Then he joined her group. As soon as she saw his evil eyes, she knew the rumor was true. This was not someone to be trifled with.

Frightened, she left the room and hurried to the cloakroom to get her jacket. She found it empty. Not desiring to stay a moment longer in that wicked atmosphere, she entered the small room full of coats and bags, searching for her windbreaker, her heart pounding madly with fear. Only the prickling of hairs on her neck gave her warning that she was not alone.

She whirled with a gasp and came face to face with the blond man—with the Devil. His body filled the doorway, blocking her only means of escape, and his cold blue eyes fixed upon her. There was a small smile on his hard lips as he looked into her very soul and saw how weak and pitiful she felt, how many secret shames and petty angers she harbored. He despised them; he despised her. She was worth nothing—less than nothing— and deserved every horrible punishment he could devise for her.

Her whole body was trembling and her knees buckled underneath her at the malevolence pulsing through the little room. Horrible images emanated from the still figure in the doorway, crowding into her paralyzed brain. She saw herself encased in a coffin, her body wrapped in chains so that she could not lash out or attempt to escape. The musty-smelling coffin had been thrust deep into the ground, and she could hear dirt being shoveled on top. Her only companion in this living nightmare was a moldering corpse, its bones cutting deep into her flesh. A tiny candle, left to torment her, was flickering madly as it sucked up the last of the air inside the coffin. Its very presence was killing her, but she despaired at the thought of losing the light. The candle flickered once, twice, and then went out, leaving her gasping hopelessly for oxygen that was no longer there.

Terrified, she thrust the images from her mind and backed away from the door, glancing around for some way to escape from this horror. Her eyes landed on a Bible that was lying among the jumble of bags on a nearby end table. She grabbed the Bible and threw it at the Devil; as it sailed through the air, their eyes locked. His gaze held her transfixed with a terror beyond conscious thought. She would be gutted alive like a fish, her organs wrenched out and exposed to the killing light of day as her blood spewed out upon the cruel ground. She would be fully aware of every wrenching pain, wishing for the mercy of death to blot the anguish.

With a piercing cry, she awoke and rolled over. It took two attempts to turn on the light. She gazed fearfully around the room, looking for a tall blond figure, but the room was empty. She lay trembling in her bed with the overhead light on until dawn, a worn Bible clenched in both hands.

The next morning was the end of term. Her parents and younger sister helped her clear out her dorm room and pack the car. It was dusk before they settled into their seats for the two-hour trip home. They talked excitedly as they drove, interrupting each other often, contradicting themselves and laughing. It was good to be together again.

They were twenty minutes from home when they left the highway. Her father turned onto Washington Rock Road, which wound up the mountain, through Washington Rock State Park, and then down the other side. The area was made into a state park to commemorate the historical events of 1777, when General George Washington had used the large namesake stone as a lookout point. From there he had a thirty-mile panoramic view of the valley and was able to circle his troops behind the British soldiers marching toward Westfield, thereby cutting off their retreat.

Her family loved this story, and they always slowed down at the top of the hill to look at the lights in the valley and the fantastic New York City skyline. But tonight was different. As the car began its ascent, she desperately wished they had chosen another route home. Growing up, she had heard dark stories about the park—rumors of human sacrifices carried out in the woods and meetings of a Satanic church on moonless nights. Utter rot, of course. But after her terrifying dream, she did not want to drive through the park at night.

A noisy motorcycle tailgated them, trying to pass even though the road was windy and narrow. Finally, the mountain grew so steep that the driver was forced to slow down, and soon they pulled away from him entirely.

The car reached the top of the mountain and started around the long curve that took them through Washington Rock State Park. The night was dark and still. The whole family automatically looked to their right, toward the New York City skyline. But instead their eyes were drawn to a small park cart sitting at the center of the bend. It was right next to the road, just inside the park boundary, and was eerily illuminated by a brilliant streetlamp that none of them had ever noticed before. Inside the vehicle . . .

She started to tremble fiercely. Inside the vehicle was a tall, handsome blond man with eyes that pierced her like a knife and held her transfixed with a terror beyond conscious thought. It was the man from her dream. The man everyone said was the Devil! The tension in the car was palpable. She had mentioned her dream to no one, but her family could feel the malevolence pulsing from the still figure in the cart. No one spoke as they drew nearer.

Suddenly, the engine gave a strange cough. Her father gunned the motor in a silent, desperate battle to keep moving. Her heart stopped for a moment with a clutch of fear that shocked her body with physical pain. She gripped her hands

ON WASHINGTON ROCK

together, praying silently as she stared at the figure opposite their car. The engine caught again and her father pressed down hard on the accelerator. Then they were past the man and roaring away from the park, toward the downward slope of the mountain.

She was sweating profusely, unable to stop shaking. She looked out the rear window at the man in the park cart, sitting ominously still beneath the brilliant light. At that moment the motorcycle appeared at the top of the hill and made its way onto the park road. As the rider drew opposite the figure in the cart, she heard the motorcycle's engine cough—and then stall. Then the park was out of view and her family was riding silently toward home, not daring to speak until they were safely indoors.

22

The Miller and the Topielec

The townsfolk said the previous miller had been lured into the millpond by a *topielec* (toe-PEE-el-ets), but I figured it was just superstitious nonsense and purchased the mill in spite of the rumors. According to town records the miller had committed suicide, and as far as I was concerned, that was the truth of the matter. A *topielec* is the spirit of a drowned human that delights in luring other people to a watery death. These creatures not only suck people into swamps and lakes, the locals say, but also kill animals standing near still waters. This is a lot of hokum, in my opinion. No intelligent man would believe in a *topielec*.

I got the mill back up and running in no time. Soon business was booming, and I found myself a plump wife and a nice set of friends. My wife and I were expecting, and I was looking forward to becoming a father for the first time.

Every now and then, someone would visit the mill and tell me a story about a *topielec* coming after this person or that, but I just laughed it off. The townsfolk were worried because I lived and worked so close to the water, but I assured them that no water-spirit had ever called to me!

Shortly after the last set of *topielec* stories ran through our community, my nephew came to stay with my wife and me while his parents traveled in Europe. He was a sturdy little chap, and he kept my wife hopping. He was always climbing trees and then falling out of them, running down the road to play with the neighbor's children, and asking question after question after question. My wife, God love her, took it all in stride. It was good practice, she told me one night. Our baby would be just as precocious when he or she grew to be our nephew's age.

Sometimes my wife brought my nephew down to the mill, where he would "help" me work. Other days, they arrived at dusk to walk home with me over the bridge and up the road to the large, fancy home I had bought for my pretty wife. It was a little too big for just us two, but the baby would soon fix that.

One evening at dusk, I was tidying up the mill in preparation for closing when I heard a terrible scream from outside. I dropped everything and ran for the door, reaching it just as my wife and nephew burst into the mill. My wife was wet to her knees and hysterical. My nephew was soaked almost to his neck, and he, too, was pale and trembling. I caught both of them close to me, my heart pounding in fear, and asked them what was wrong. Sobbing, my wife stammered out the story.

They had been coming down the hill toward the bridge when a voice rang out from near the millpond. Such a lovely voice, singing a song they had never heard. Entranced, my wife left the road and walked toward the water with my puzzled nephew close on her heels. A misty figure was rising from the depths of the pond, singing softly to itself and beckoning to my wife. As she drew close to the edge, the figure became clearer; it looked and sounded like an angel. Suddenly, it stopped singing and stared intently at my wife's very round belly. Then it looked at my nephew, who was crying with fear at my wife's strange behavior and trying to draw her out of the water. The creature gave a snarl of rage and disappeared abruptly beneath the water, breaking the spell on my wife.

My wife snapped out of her trance and discovered that she was knee-deep in the millpond. A few more steps would have plunged her into the deep hole near the center, my nephew with her. Because neither of them knew how to swim, they would surely have drowned. It was at that moment that my wife had screamed and run from the water, clutching my nephew to her chest.

I was stunned and speechless. I did not believe in water-spirits, but my wife was a truthful woman, and I had no other explanation for what had happened to her. I hurried my wife and nephew home and drew a hot bath for each of them. Once they were warm and comfortable, I made them some dinner and then put them both to bed. I made my wife promise that she would not go near the millpond again at dusk, a promise she readily made.

When both my wife and my nephew were asleep, I crossed the street to talk to my neighbor, who was the first person to tell me about the *topielec*. He listened soberly to my story and then explained that water-spirits are afraid of children and pregnant women because the innocence of youths and unborn babes saves them from the siren-like *topielec*'s song. God gave children a special protection against the forces of evil, a defense that older and wiser adults do not have. This was why the *topielec* had broken off its song and released my wife from its coils.

THE MILLER AND THE TOPIELEC

My wife and nephew had been very lucky, the neighbor told me, but I should take extra precautions from then on. Now that the *topielec* had awakened, it would be looking for another victim. I could not laugh off his warning this time. My neighbor advised me to carry a cross or some other holy object at all times, and if a *topielec* ever came near me, to show that object to the creature and bid it go away in the name of God.

The very next day I purchased three crosses. I hung one around my wife's neck and one around my nephew's, giving strict instructions regarding their use should the *topielec* reappear. The third cross I kept in my pocket, just in case.

Nearly a month passed without incident. I began to relax again, hoping that the *topielec* had gone back to sleep. The baby was due in a few weeks, and I was putting in a lot of overtime at the mill to square away most of my accounts.

One evening around midnight, I was in my office finishing up the last of the paperwork when the door behind me blew open with a bang. I dropped my pen, startled by the noise as a blast of cold and clammy air whirled about the room. I could hear footsteps coming up the stairs. I turned in my chair and saw a misty shape standing in the doorway. It twisted and undulated strangely, as if it were made of water, and seaweed swirled about its head like green strands of hair. The figure beckoned to me. Beautiful, enticing music echoed in the room, and it seemed that I had to follow the melody where it led. I half rose from my chair, but some vestige of sense sent me groping in my pocket for the cross. I pulled it out and held it toward the watery figure. The creature became still, and the music faded to a whisper.

"In the name of God, I bid you to go away. Never bother me or my family again," I gasped.

The *topielec* turned in silence and undulated down the stairs and out of the mill. The cold and clammy air went with it, leaving me shaking but alive. My clothes were soaking wet, and small puddles of water that looked strangely like footprints led down from my office, through the mill, and out to the pond.

When I got home that night, my wife screamed at the sight of me. I looked in the mirror in the front hall and saw that my dark hair had turned snow-white. She demanded an explanation, and I reluctantly told her about my confrontation with the *topielec*. The agitation caused by my story brought on labor pains, and my son was born a few hours later.

From that day forward my wife, nephew, son, and I always carried crosses to guard us against the water-spirits. We never saw a *topielec* again.

23

The Express Train to Hell

Pa drove us to the train station in his new buggy, much to the delight of my small son, who sat in the seat beside him and "helped" him drive. Ma wanted to come with us, but she was so pale by the time we finished serving dessert that Pa and I both insisted she go straight to bed. Ma had felt poorly for some time, and my wife and I visited as often as we could with our children.

It was late when we left my folks' place and later still when we finally boarded the train for home. Timmy, who had just turned four, lay against my shoulder, fast asleep. Baby Cecily was awake in my wife's arms, cooing contentedly. Her grandma had been right pleased to see the little tyke, and I didn't regret lingering over a late dinner. I wasn't sure how much longer Ma would be with us, and I wanted to make the most of the time we had left.

My folks had asked us to stay the night with them, but I needed to be at work early in the morning, so Hannah and I had declined their invitation. It was nearly midnight when we pulled into Newark Central Station, where we had to switch trains. I settled Hannah and the children in a seat near the tracks and

158

navigated my way through the crowd to look for a timetable. I quickly discovered that the next train to home didn't leave until 12:15 a.m. *Good thing I found a seat for Hannah and the kids,* I thought as I hurried back toward my family.

Suddenly, a ragged old man leapt out of the crowd and seized the lapel of my jacket.

"It's coming for me!" he shrieked into my face, with breath that stank of alcohol. "It's coming!"

"Now see here, fella," I exclaimed, trying to pull him off.

"I done wrong!" the man said, his fingers digging painfully into my chest. "I killed a man who cheated me at cards, and now I'm going to pay!"

"Get off me," I cried, pushing him as hard as I could. He was unnaturally strong for such a wiry little man. He pressed his wrinkled face close to mine, and I was nearly overpowered by his terrible stench. He surely had not washed anytime this decade.

"It's coming for me!" he roared. "The Express Train for Hell is coming for my soul! You've got to help me."

At that moment the stationmaster and several men came to my rescue, pulling the old man away and apologizing profusely.

"I'm so sorry, sir," the stationmaster said, brushing dirt from my coat. "That old tramp has been here for the last several days. We keep chasing him off the property, but he sneaks back when we aren't looking. He's crazy but harmless. Can I get you a drink, or escort you to a seat?"

"No, no, I'm fine," I said. After murmuring several more reassurances, I managed to break away from the stationmaster and rejoin Hannah and the children.

"What was that about?" asked Hannah, who had observed the encounter but was too far away to hear the exchange between myself and the tramp.

"Some crazy old guy wanted me to save him from the 'Express Train to Hell,'" I told her. "He seemed to think it was coming for him because he'd killed a man who was cheating him at cards."

"That's terrible," Hannah said. She shuddered and hugged the baby closer. I picked up little Timmy, who lay asleep by her side, and settled him into my lap without waking him.

"The stationmaster said he's been hanging around here for days. They will probably have to call the police if he keeps accosting people," I added.

I leaned against the back of the seat and gazed out over the darkened tracks. The 11:50 train blew its whistle, and a hiss of steam accompanied it as it chugged away from the station. I yawned, wishing that our train would come quickly. It had been a long, stressful day. I found it hard to watch Ma's declining health, especially when there was nothing any of us could do to save her. Hannah leaned against me and shut her eyes.

At two minutes to midnight, we were both awakened by terrible shouting.

"It's coming for me! It's coming!" The old tramp leapt onto the platform a few feet away from us. "The Express Train for Hell is coming for my soul!"

All over the platform, dozing passengers sat up and looked around sleepily for the source of the noise. Then a new sound introduced itself—a long whistle blowing once, twice. I was startled. The next train wasn't due until 12:05. *It must be arriving early,* I thought.

THE EXPRESS TRAIN TO HELL

The old tramp started screaming again when he heard the whistle. We could hear the roar and chug of a steam train, approaching fast. Approaching *too fast* to stop at the station.

It's a runaway, I thought, jumping up with Timmy in my arms and grabbing Hannah and the baby. As I dragged them away from our seat near the tracks, the stationmaster and his two helpers ran onto the platform and took hold of the old tramp.

The whistle sounded again. A warm rush of air blew against everyone near the platform as an invisible train passed directly in front of us. We heard the hiss of the steam and the screech of flanges against iron rails; we felt the wind whipping our hair and faces. But we saw nothing. I blinked in amazement.

To my left the old tramp gave a terrible wail. Then he vanished, leaving the two station assistants empty-handed. The noise of the invisible train faded into the distance and then ceased. Baby Cecily woke up and started whimpering, her little voice the only sound on the now-quiet platform. I glanced at the station clock. It was midnight.

One of the assistants broke the eerie silence. "Where did he go? He was right here! I had him in my hands! *Where did he go?*"

The stationmaster was staring blankly at the tracks. "Good Lord, he was right. It did come for him," he said aloud. He pulled out a handkerchief and wiped his sweating, bald head with it.

"What came for him?" shouted the hysterical assistant.

"The Express Train to Hell," said the stationmaster. He shook his head and that seemed to bring him to his senses. "Get a hold of yourself, man," he added crisply to his assistant.

"You and George go back into the station and pour yourselves a drink."

He pushed the two men through the station door. Then, noticing the dazed and frightened passengers, he turned and said, "Nothing to worry about, folks. It was just an express train passing through. The next train will be here in five minutes."

The stationmaster's reassuring manner calmed everyone. People turned away from the empty tracks and settled back into their seats, whispering to each other about the strange events that had just taken place.

"Did I just see what I think I saw?" asked Hannah.

"If you mean an invisible train running through this station and picking up a passenger for Hell, then yes, you did," I replied.

Another train whistle drowned out the last few words. Everyone on the platform shrieked and leapt to their feet in fear, but a moment later a very real headlight illuminated the midnight darkness and the reassuringly solid bulk of a steam engine pulled slowly up to the platform. The conductor dismounted and several passengers shuffled off the 12:05 a.m. train.

Cautiously, the large family that had been seated next to us approached the train. The mother felt all along the side of the passenger car to make sure it was real before she allowed her sleepy children to board.

The conductor shook his head and said to me, "You see all sorts of strange things in this job. That lady acts as if she doesn't believe the train is solid!" He returned to his post, still shaking his head, and the train slowly moved off.

"I want to go home," Hannah said, huddling into the crook of my arm. "I don't want to stay in this crazy, haunted station."

"Me neither," I said, holding her close.

We waited in silence until our own train pulled in, and then I swept my family inside, vowing to take a different route home next time. I never wanted to see the Express Train to Hell again.

As our train chugged away from Newark Central, I glanced back at the dark platform and felt a sudden stab of pity for the poor old tramp. Then I wondered if there was an Express Train to Heaven. If so, I knew that was the train that would come for my Ma someday soon.

The White Stag

SHAMONG, BURLINGTON COUNTY

James did not like the look of the weather. Storm clouds were threatening overhead, moving in an ominously circular motion; the evening air had a strange, greenish tinge; and the wind had picked up. Twisters had threatened his stagecoach run more than once.

A brilliant flash of lightning lit the faces of his passengers as they climbed aboard the stagecoach. A mother and her two small children were joined by a businessman and a bearded chap with a nautical air whom James silently dubbed "the captain." It was a longish ride to their destination, the Quaker Bridge Inn over in Shamong, and James was afraid it was going to be a cold and wet journey, at least for him and the horses.

He adjusted the last of the baggage, settled into his seat on top of the carriage, and gathered up the reins. The horses were jittery and danced a little in their traces as a loud clap of thunder followed another bolt of lightning. The air was damp and heavy. *Well, the sooner started, the sooner ended,* James mused to himself, pulling his hat down around his ears and snapping the reins. The horses shuddered a bit and moved forward with a jingle of bits.

Less than a mile into their journey, the rain began. First came a few large, heavy drops that stung the back of James's neck and made him pull up his muffler. Soon they gave way to a torrential downpour that swept over the woods and turned the road into a muddy nightmare. The horses sweated and strained as the mud grew deeper and the rain continued. James was reminded of his travel in the tropics, where he had worked as a sailor for a few years—only the rain in the tropics was much warmer than in New Jersey. He pulled his great coat tighter around his thin frame and urged the horses onward.

James could make out the sound of grumbling protests from inside the swaying stagecoach as the passengers were flung from one side to the other. A terrible wind was whipping fiercely against the coach, rattling the ropes that held down the luggage and turning James's hands to ice. He heard the children cry out in fear and frustration as the storm continued to thunder around them. James wanted to howl himself, as Quaker Bridge and its inn were still several miles away. He urged the horses forward, shaking the water off the brim of his hat, wanting the journey to be over quickly. His only thought was for a warm drink and a soft bed to sleep in.

Suddenly, the wind began a strange, swirling dance around the stagecoach, which swung so far to the right that it almost toppled over. James clung tightly to the reins with one hand and to his wooden seat with the other, leaning to the left as hard as he could to help tip the coach upright. The horses strained forward, whinnying in fright as the coach landed again on all four wheels.

James glanced upward. A funnel was forming in the sky above them. He gave a shout of terror and whipped the reins fiercely, but the horses needed no urging; sensing the danger they leapt forward, dragging the stagecoach along the muddy road as if it were made of cobbles or dry earth. James could do nothing but hang on and pray as they bolted forward, sweeping through the dark forest and torrential rain, heading for higher ground near the bridge.

James risked a glance behind him during the next lightning flare and saw a deadly finger reaching down from a gray-green cloud, stretching toward the place where they had been only a few moments before. He gulped, looking ahead again and gritting his teeth against the terrible strain on his arms as he tried to control the fleeing horses. He could no longer hear the voices of the passengers. They, too, were probably hanging on for dear life and praying.

A few tense minutes later, the roar of the wind died down somewhat, and the horses slowed. James gasped with relief. He glanced behind him again but could see nothing save the shadowy shape of rain-lashed trees in the darkness. He glanced upward during the next flash of lightning, but the twister had disappeared. He relaxed a bit more into the seat.

The trees were thinning in front of him, and he could hear the sound of rushing water. They were almost to Quaker Bridge. Straining his eyes against the rainy darkness, James could make out a light in the distance. *That must be the inn,* he thought. He urged the horses forward, his eyes focused on the light on the far bank.

Suddenly, a huge white form leapt from the trees ahead and flung itself into the path of the stagecoach. The horses screamed with terror, twisting in their traces, dancing sideways and then rearing. James fought desperately for control as the stagecoach pitched from side to side. His arms were throbbing with pain, but he finally managed to pull the horses to a stop.

James stared in bemused shock at the glowing blur in the road before him. It was a giant white stag. He blinked. One of his buddies, a member of the Lenape tribe, sometimes talked about a white deer that was supposed to be good luck, but James had never believed his stories. Who had ever heard of a white deer?

Yet the beautiful stag in front of him was real. He had never seen such a large creature. It stared at him as if it could read his mind, and it showed no fear of the sweating, snorting horses or of James. Nor did it show any sign of leaving the road.

James could hear "the captain" bellowing questions up at him. Ignoring the nautical man and his colorful language, James jumped down from the stagecoach and walked through the drilling rain toward the white stag.

"I'm sorry, my proud fellow, but you are going to have to move out of the way," he said as he approached the animal. "We've just had a bad scare, and we need to get to the inn."

The white stag looked deeply into his eyes for a moment. And then it vanished. James gasped. Where had the creature gone? One moment it stood less than a yard away from him, as still as a statue with its white coat glittering in the rain, and the next moment the road was empty. His eye had been on the beast the entire time, and he had not seen it run away.

James glanced around in amazement. Then he froze as his eye fell on the bridge, just a few paces beyond where the white stag had stood. Not far from the bank, the bridge had collapsed into the raging waters of the vastly engorged river below it. From his driver's perch on the stagecoach, James would not

THE WHITE STAG

have seen the breakage until it was too late to stop the coach from plummeting into the torrent.

James started shaking in horror as he realized that the white stag had just saved him and his passengers from drowning. He staggered back to the stagecoach, pausing for a moment to calm the horses. Then he opened the door to the coach and told the passengers why he had stopped. The two men inside clambered down to help James warn the innkeeper of the bridge's collapse. Together, they took lanterns to the bank of the river, where they shouted and signaled until they received a response from the inn. Then they set up a temporary roadblock so that no one else would try to use the collapsed bridge. Finally, James turned the stagecoach around, drove it down to the next crossing, and then back up the far side of the river to drop off his passengers at the Quaker Bridge Inn.

James's story of the white stag was met with much amazement and some skepticism. It spread rapidly through the town and then all over the countryside. Though rarely seen again, the phantom white stag was ever after considered good luck by everyone living and traveling in the Pine Barrens, from that day to this.

25

Blackbeard's Treasure

Joel first heard the rumors about the large black walnut tree when he visited the local tavern in his new hometown. The tree was located on Wood Street, and it was said to be the haunt of witches who met late at night, chanting and dancing and working foul magic. It was best, people told him, not to walk down Wood Street on nights when the moon was full. He thought it all nonsense, of course. Just local folklore. But it was amusing to listen to the stories, nonetheless.

There came a week of terrible storms, and no one ventured out unless they absolutely had to. After the storms had blown themselves to sea, Teddy, the town drunk, stumbled into the local tavern with a wild new story about the black walnut tree. Late one dark and stormy night, he had seen some scurvy-looking chaps sneak into the port on a ship that bore no flag. Finding this suspicious, he watched the men without being seen and realized that they were the very worst sort of pirates. Soon they were joined on deck by a tall, flamboyant captain with a long beard. Teddy recognized him at once—it was the notorious Blackbeard!

The pirates lugged several treasure chests off the ship and disappeared behind the black walnut tree, presumably burying them beneath its roots. When the deed was done, Blackbeard took a gun and loaded into it a "charmed" bullet. This bullet, he told his companions, would allow a dead man to return and fight off anyone who might come after the treasure. Before they could absorb this information, the bold captain spun around and shot one of his men in the chest. The others gasped and jumped backward as the dead pirate tumbled to the ground. They dragged his body away, presumably to bury it with the treasure chests. Then the pirates went back to their ship, leaving the ghost of their dead companion behind to guard the loot.

"Sure, and if that be true, why are you here telling us about this incident when you could be at the black walnut tree, digging up buried treasure?" called the bartender.

"I would be, except when I went out there with my shovel, who should be dancing around the tree but old Meg and her witches!" Teddy said with boozy dignity. "They were chanting up a curse on the pirates who dared to defile their meeting place. None of those pirates will make it home alive after this venture if old Meg has anything to say about it!"

It was obvious from the way everyone was laughing and joking about the treasure that no one believed a word the town drunk was saying. Nevertheless, Joel was intrigued. Tales of buried treasure were more likely to circulate among the shore communities in New Jersey. However, a clever pirate captain might claim that his treasure was buried near the sea when it actually was buried inland near a river port. By all accounts, Blackbeard was no fool.

After the tavern closed for the night, Joel sought out the town drunk and asked him for details. Teddy was happy to supply them, feeling vindicated now that this clever young man believed his story. The pirates, he said, had laid a large flat stone over the place they buried the treasure. He could show Joel the spot, but they had to split the treasure equally between them. Joel agreed.

Not wanting anyone to get a jump on them, Joel collected two shovels, some candles, and a lantern from his home and hurried Teddy over to Wood Street. It was partially cloudy that night. The full moon kept appearing and disappearing behind the clouds as they passed under the giant black walnut tree. Spying a flat rock nearby, Joel went over to it and set down his lantern. Teddy peered around blurrily and said, "I'm not sure this is the right place."

"You said a flat rock by the black walnut tree," Joel said impatiently. He wondered why he had dragged this drunken fool along with him.

The two men began to dig. Joel was not used to manual labor of this sort, so he left the bulk of the work to his companion, who was humming happily to himself and pausing to take a few drags at his "medicinal" bottle of whisky.

They had dug quite a deep hole before Teddy's shovel clanged against something solid. Joel leapt neatly down into the cavity, where he began digging with enthusiasm. To his disgust, his shovel turned over only a large rock. As he pushed it aside, the bottom of the hole suddenly gave way beneath them. With a shout of surprise, Joel and Teddy plunged into a large underground cavern that lay beneath the black walnut tree.

It was pitch black in the cavern, and it echoed strangely whenever Joel moved. Remembering the candles he had shoved in his pockets, Joel scrambled to his feet, lit one, and peered around him in wonder. No one in town had ever spoken of caverns under the black walnut tree—or anywhere else, for that matter. This was an old formation, filled with mighty stalactites stretching down toward tall stalagmites underneath them. The air was damp and chilly.

He turned around, looking for Teddy, and then stopped and stared. Near the far wall were three large black sea chests. *Good Lord,* he thought. *There really is treasure here!*

Forgetting all about Teddy, Joel hurried over to the chests. He broke open the lock on the middle trunk, using a rock he found on the floor. Inside, a mass of gold coins, jewels, and other precious objects shone. Joel drew in his breath and held it, for a jaunty whistle began to echo through the cavern, along with the sound of boots stomping merrily toward him. He grabbed a handful of jewels and gold coins, stuffing them into his pockets. Then he threw himself behind a stalagmite just as a strange, greenish light sprang up to his right. A tall man with wicked black eyes, the handsome clothing of a wealthy pirate, and a long, fancy beard entered the cavern. It was Blackbeard.

The pirate approached his treasure chests but stopped short, staring at the one in the center. Joel covered his mouth to suppress a gasp. He had forgotten to close the lid! Blackbeard drew his cutlass slowly from his side, a terrible smile lighting up that wicked face.

"All right, where are ye laddies?" he called. "Come out and see your captain, if you dare!"

BLACKBEARD'S TREASURE

At that moment Teddy groaned and sat up among the debris that had descended with them into the cavern. Blackbeard whirled toward the sound. Joel stared at the pirate confronting his drunken companion, and then over at the open treasure chest. He sighed inwardly. *It is too bad I am an honorable man,* he thought, bounding forward with a shout.

When Blackbeard turned, searching for the source of the loud cry, Joel grabbed Teddy by his collar and dragged him to his feet. Joel could feel gold coins and gem stones spilling from his pockets as he ran down a long, dark passageway that eventually dumped them onto the riverbank. The two men did not stop running until they reached Joel's house, where they fortified themselves by finishing all the whisky in Teddy's bottle.

Just before sunrise they crept back to the black walnut tree to retrieve their shovels and the lantern. They found their equipment right where they had left it, but the ground at the base of the tree was completely undisturbed. When they returned to the riverbank to look for the passageway leading to the underground cavern, it was gone.

Teddy declared that the whole thing had been a strange dream brought on by too much drink, but Joel was not so sure. Thinking back on Teddy's story, he realized that the black walnut tree mentioned by the town drunk had not necessarily been the one on Wood Street. Teddy had probably been down by the river the night Blackbeard came with his men. He most likely had watched the pirates going into the cavern with their treasure chests. In his drunken state, he had mixed up this story with one about Old Meg and the witch's tree. There must, Joel decided, be a black walnut tree somewhere near the entrance to the caves. The fact that the cavern used by the pirates was directly under the tree on Wood Street was a serendipitous coincidence. And the undisturbed ground by the tree could easily be explained—Blackbeard probably had noticed the gaping hole in the roof and sent his men to fill it.

Joel spent the rest of the fall searching for a way back into the cavern. At first he thought to dig his way back in, so he took his shovel to the black walnut tree on Wood Street and started excavating. He was interrupted by the high-pitched cackling of Old Meg. Startled, he dropped the shovel and found himself looking deep into the old witch's eyes.

"Looking for something, sonny?" she asked softly, fingering her cane with long, twisted fingers. His mouth suddenly dry, Joel could only nod, hypnotized by Old Meg's fierce stare.

"You'd best leave this place alone, if you want to stay healthy and whole," she said menacingly. She swung the cane suddenly toward Joel's head. He ducked just in time, then picked up his shovel and ran away, followed by the witch's laughter.

After that Joel did not dare return to the black walnut tree on Wood Street for fear that Old Meg would curse him. He spent his free time near the river instead, seeking the place where he and Teddy had emerged from the cavern depths. It took him several months to locate the entrance, which, as he suspected, was near a black walnut tree.

Following his triumphant rediscovery, Joel spent many days exploring a large cavern full of stalactites and stalagmites. It might have been the one he and Teddy fell into—except there was nothing inside it but rocks. Blackbeard had probably cleared out his treasure as soon as he realized interlopers had discovered the cave, Joel finally decided one afternoon. At that moment a glimmer caught his eye. Walking over to the place where the chests had stood, he stooped down with his lantern. Lying on the floor was one solid-gold coin. Joel picked it up and turned it over and over in his hand. "So it wasn't a dream," he mused.

Joel kept the coin as a good-luck token the rest of his life, but he never told anyone where he found it—just in case the pirates returned someday to bury their hoard inside the cavern once more.

26

The Devil's Duets

I reckon there wasn't any fiddler in the world that could play better than Sammy Giberson. He was a merry fellow who played at all the social gatherings in the Pinelands. Folks just loved having him around. Now, Sammy liked his "Jersey Lightning" (that's what folks hereabouts call the Pineland applejack), and after a few drinks he would get tipsy and start boasting that no man could best him at fiddlin'. Since he was so good, hardly anyone tried.

But Bill Dunn, he was different. He was a fancy violin player, not so popular as Sammy but real good with a fiddle. He didn't like Sammy's attitude. One night, when Bill was drinking at the tavern near New Gretna, he heard Sammy boasting of his fiddling skills, and something in him snapped. Right then and there, Bill whipped out his own fiddle and challenged Sammy to a duel.

Well, those two fellows went at it like a house afire. They fiddled and danced and fiddled some more, pausing just long enough to take a swig of applejack on account of the terrible thirst they worked up with all that playing. By the end of the evening, they were both pretty tipsy, but neither one was willing to concede the contest to the other. So the rest of the folks in the tavern stepped in and voted Sammy the winner.

Sammy stood on top of a chair and took a swaying bow with his instrument clasped to his chest. "I could best the Devil himself at fiddlin'!" he boasted to the lads who hurriedly helped him down from the chair before he fell off and broke his fiddle. Bill shook his head when he heard this boast and muttered something to the effect that Sammy should watch what he wished for. Sammy laughed at him, and the rest of the customers thought Bill's prediction was just the poor-spirited grumblings of a loser. They were all wrong.

As Sammy staggered home through the woods that balmy summer night, he suddenly came face-to-face with a mysterious, dark stranger.

"Sammy Giberson?" the man asked.

"Yer talkin' to him!" Sammy said, blinking at the man and taking a quick nip from his flask of applejack to steady his nerves.

"I hear you can play the fiddle better than the Devil," said the stranger.

"That's right," Sammy said, waving his fiddle case at the mystery man.

"Prove it," said the dark stranger, flinging back his cloak to reveal the sharply wicked face of the Devil himself. He tucked a fiddle under his chin and started playing a melody of such heartbreaking sweetness that Sammy wanted to weep. Instead, he pulled out his own fiddle and countered with a rollicking tune that made the Devil's toes tap.

Well, the Pinelands rang that night with song after song—some sad, some sweet, some humorous, and some so haunting that they could steal away your soul. The Devil and Sammy were

THE DEVIL'S DUETS

musical equals. At sunrise the Devil nodded his head to Sammy and invited him to another fiddling session the next evening. Sammy agreed, and old Lucifer disappeared in a puff of smoke.

Sammy couldn't remember an evening he had enjoyed more. He tucked his fiddle under one arm and strolled home, still humming the last tune the Devil had played. What a song! Perhaps the Devil would teach it to him, he thought.

The next night and many nights thereafter, Sammy met the Devil deep in the Pinelands. They would laugh and chat and play duets together, first Sammy taking the melody and then the Devil. Folks strolling in the moonlight often remarked on the wonderful sounds that came from the woods as the Devil and Sammy wove melody and harmony into a sound so amazing that it could bring tears to the eyes of the most hardened criminal.

Sammy pestered the dark lord to teach him all the tunes the Devil had played on the night of their first duel. The most haunting of these melodies was called simply "the air tune." It became the most requested song in the Pinelands. Sammy would play it only at the close of each evening, and only after fortifying himself with some Jersey Lightning. Something about the song reminded people of their first love or their baby's first smile or the first sunset they had ever seen. When folks asked Sammy where he had learned the beautiful tune, he told them he had just picked it "out of the air" one night when he was walking home from the tavern near New Gretna. That was the only time Sammy ever alluded to his encounters with the Devil.

Folks all over the Pinelands were brokenhearted when Sammy died. Some said that the night he passed away, a lone violin could be heard out in the woods playing the air tune as a dirge for Sammy Giberson. People claimed that it was the

Devil himself who played that evening, mourning the loss of the talented fiddler who was his duet partner and friend. A few cynical people said this was just plumb nonsense. They said that Sammy had as good as sold his soul to the Devil when they started playing together—that the Devil must have taken Sammy's soul as a payment for all the music he had taught the fiddler.

A few weeks after he was buried in the cemetery in Little Egg Harbor, Sammy's fiddle took to playing all by itself in its case. His friends recognized the sweet strains it played as the air tune. They were mighty spooked by the sound, and they didn't know whether to be sad or relieved when the fiddle disappeared into thin air one night in late autumn.

Shortly thereafter, a young couple walking hand in hand through the Pinelands on a beautiful moonlit night heard the sound of two fiddles playing deep in the heart of the forest. They claimed that Sammy's ghost had returned to the land he loved to make music with the Devil. To this day, if you travel in the Pinelands under moonlight, you might catch a few notes of a tune that reminds you of your first love or your baby's first smile or the first sunset you ever saw. If you do, keep an eye out for Sammy, who is still playing duets with his old pal the Devil.

27

The Grim

WEST MILFORD

I normally don't go for spooky adventures, being too busy trying to earn a college scholarship to take time off from my studies. But when I heard that Rob was going up to the bonfire on Clinton Road, I decided to go along for the ride. I was impressed with Rob. He was fairly new to our school, having joined our class halfway through our junior year. It was now October of our senior year, and he had already won a full scholarship to Harvard University. But Rob also liked to have fun, and I admired that in a man. I was the intelligent-but-shy type; an outgoing "brainiac" was my kind of guy.

Rob and I had been eyeing each other all fall, and so I wasn't too surprised when he casually took my hand as the gang was leaving our favorite pizza place and told the others that I would be riding up to Clinton Road in his car. Rob was driving an old yellow Mustang that he had restored himself. A soon-to-be Harvard student who could restore cars—what a guy! He actually opened the passenger door for me and made sure I was comfortable before starting the engine.

It was a beautiful, starry night with just a sliver of a moon. As we followed the others up the mountain, Rob and I talked about our dreams and our goals for the future. We didn't talk much about Clinton Road, although we both had heard the stories.

Clinton Road was a spooky ten-mile stretch between Route 23 and Upper Greenwood Lake. It curved and dipped and twisted through desolate woodland, passing a shining lake and old abandoned furnaces, swooping in and out of a mysterious forest with blockaded paths. In the daytime it was a wonderful place to go hiking. But at night . . .

Well, I've heard the stories all my life. Night is when Satanic cults roam the woods, looking for victims to sacrifice. Night is when the ghost of a little boy who fell over the bridge at Dead Man's Curve appears near the spot of his death. (One of my friends claims that she once threw a quarter over the bridge, and that someone threw it back up to her—and there was no one else there at the time!) Night is when the witches hold their dances on Green Island.

I shivered as we turned onto Clinton Road just behind our friends' car. The only illumination came from our headlights. The trees crowded close to the edge of the road, their branches stretching out toward us like bony hands; most of them were bare in the cool October air.

We pulled off the road near the remains of Cross Castle. Rob helped me out and kept hold of my hand as we followed the group back to their favorite bonfire spot on the castle grounds. The guys quickly got a fire going, and we crowded close, happily creeped out by the darkness, the terrible reputation of the road, and the delicious feeling of being out very late at night. Rob put his arm around me as the guys started telling stories about unidentified bodies dumped on the road by the Mafia and about the corpse left in a plastic bag by the Iceman murderer. One girl spoke about late-night meetings of the KKK on the very ground we occupied.

Then my friend Katie talked about several people who were rumored to have strange visions or had seizures when they visited Cross Castle. Fortunately, our group was not suffering from any such problems—though some of the guys were getting a little silly.

The air grew colder, making me shiver. Rob noticed and tightened his arm around me, asking, "Are you okay, Madison?" My teeth were chattering, so I just nodded and kept my mouth shut, not wanting to break up the friendly group.

Little wisps of cloud had been darting across the sky above us. Soon a larger cloud obscured the sliver of moon, and the darkness around us deepened. I gazed apprehensively into the forest, rubbing my arms. I was about as close to the fire as you could get without being burned, but the flames did not warm me.

I blinked my eyes a few times and shivered again. I could swear that someone—or something—was watching us. I glanced toward the dark trees at the edge of the clearing and froze in terror. A pair of glowing red eyes was staring at the group from deep in the shadows among the trees.

"R-R-Rob!" I managed to gasp through my chattering teeth. He looked where I was pointing and then grabbed me so tightly that I temporarily lost the circulation in my arms.

"Good Lord!" he cried.

Everyone turned to look, first at Rob and then at the source of our panic. The figure of a large beast loomed, its red eyes slowly moving closer. They were widely spaced and far enough

THE GRIM

off the ground to be the eyes of a bear—but I knew this creature was not a bear. It was a huge black dog with a foaming mouth over vicious, long teeth and eyes that gleamed with the fires of death.

Suddenly the overgrown beast threw back its head and howled, challenging us for blatantly trespassing on its turf. The sound chilled my blood even as it unfroze my limbs.

"Let's get out of here!" I shrieked. Rob grabbed my hand and dragged me down the path as fast as he could run. Our friends were close on our heels as the creature pursued us. It ran like the wind, snarling and yelping and snapping at the heels of the slowest. Rob and I were not among them. He threw me into the car, clambered in after me, and took off fast. But then he steered the car back toward the woods.

"What are you doing?" I shouted in terror.

"Giving them time to escape," Rob replied grimly as our headlights picked out the monstrous black dog chasing our friends. The dog turned when it saw the lights, the gleam of its red eyes matching their brightness. It howled again, a sound that has since haunted my dreams, and lunged toward the Mustang. I saw our friends leap into their car and take off with squealing tires just before the dog slammed against the front of our car. Rob backed up as quickly as he could, frantically trying to reach the road. The motion threw the dog off the car momentarily, but it followed us and attacked the front and sides of the Mustang with renewed hatred. I came eye to eye with the creature as it smashed itself against my window.

Then we were out on the road. Rob gunned the motor and sped down that dark, twisty, ominous path. The black hound followed us, keeping up with supernatural ease and occasionally throwing its heavy bulk against the car on first one side then the other. The Mustang was going to be ruined regardless of whether we made it off of Clinton Road alive.

Rob hit a straight stretch and pumped the gas. With a last terrible howl, the hound abandoned the chase, standing in the middle of the road and watching us with those glowing red eyes. They lit up the night until we turned a bend and the dog disappeared from view.

I lay back against my seat, panting with terror as Rob frantically drove us over dips and curves and twists and potholes and out to safety. He slowed the car when we turned off Clinton Road but didn't stop. In a rather high-pitched tone, Rob asked me to grab my cell phone and see if the others were safe. I managed to reach Katie, who was hysterical with fright. After taking a few calming breaths, she assured me that no one in her vehicle was hurt and that they were all going home. I told her that we would do the same.

Rob didn't stop until we reached my house. He sat for a moment, his body trembling; then he switched off the car engine and turned to me. "Are you all right?" he asked, brushing the hair away from my cheek.

"I'm all right," I reassured him shakily. "What was that thing?"

"I think it was a Grim," Rob said.

I shook my head. "A what?"

"A Grim," Rob repeated. "A Grim is a phantom black dog that acts as a spiritual guardian, protecting the dead from disturbance by the living. Grims often haunt cemeteries, but they also have been seen on roadways used for funeral processions. Considering the number of bodies that have been dumped on

Clinton Road, I think it could be counted as a cemetery of sorts. The dog *did* seem more intent on chasing us off its territory than on killing us. I mean, it had more than one chance to drag us away."

"It sure did a job on your beautiful car," I said ruefully.

"I'm just glad everyone got away safely," Rob said. But as he spoke, he hurriedly got out to inspect the damage. I grinned discreetly at this sign of male psychology and followed him. Rob was standing under the street light, staring at the car in amazement. There was absolutely no damage, even though the doors had been repeatedly slammed by the Grim's large body.

The whole world went a little dim, and I swayed. Rob leapt to the sidewalk and caught me just before I fainted. I was out only for a moment. Then I opened my eyes and looked into his shocked face.

"Madison!" he gasped.

I drew in a deep breath and sat up. "I'm okay," I said unsteadily. I took another breath and added, "Look, Rob, the next time we go out, why don't we just see a movie?"

He gave me a big hug and agreed.

28

Gully Road

NEWARK

He had wanted to be a sailor all his life, and no amount of advice from his good mother and father could dissuade him. Eventually they agreed to let him work on a schooner that sailed out of the port of Newark and was captained by a man who lived in their neighborhood. It was to be a trial run, no more. If the captain was pleased with his abilities, then the lad might sign on permanently as the second mate. If not, he would put aside this sailing nonsense and go to work in his father's store. That was the deal to which he had agreed.

The sailing life was not easy, but the young man took to it as a duck takes to water. He soon grew as tough as the old salts manning the captain's schooner, with taut muscles and a swaggering air about him. The only thing he found difficult to bear was the captain's habit of cursing from morning to night. The youngster's parents were very religious—swearing was just not done at his house. The other sailors cussed a bit here and there over their work, but the captain didn't seem to know how to form a sentence without several swearwords included. The lad's ears turned red sometimes to hear him.

The voyage went very well indeed, and the captain offered to train the young man and make a proper second mate of him. The recruit agreed immediately, and the captain promised to speak to his parents about his potential.

They were almost home when a terrible storm broke, causing the ship to thrash from side to side relentlessly. It took all of the captain's skill to bring the schooner safely into the port of Newark. Over the howling, thrashing wind, the captain bade the men—with many a curse about the weather—to go home for the night. They could return after the storm ended to unload the ship. Pleased, the men scurried off, bound for drier quarters.

"Come along, then," the captain said as he steered the young sailor toward their own homes in Bellevue.

It was a long, weary walk at any time of day, but on a night such as this, it was a horrendous experience. Only the longing to see his good parents and tell them how well he had done on his first voyage kept the young sailor moving through the driving rain and the mud. Thunder rumbled, lightning flashed, and the wind roared around them as they staggered homeward. The young man and the old captain clutched their storm gear close to them, and the captain kept up a steady stream of cursing that made his recruit blush in embarrassment. He fervently hoped that the captain would tone it down when they reached his parents' house.

At first the young sailor was too busy fighting the storm to notice his surroundings. Then he realized with horror that instead of following the regular route toward Bellevue, the captain was taking a shortcut. No matter what the weather, the young man would have never considered this path, for it led them straight down Gully Road.

He'd heard the stories about the dark, narrow road since childhood. There were folks—including his own parents—who wouldn't walk down Gully Road in broad daylight, not even if they were accompanied by the local minister carrying holy water and a Bible. An elderly couple was said to haunt the road, searching for their old cottage, which was destroyed by the town in order to widen the road. People also claimed to see the ghost of a Tory who was hanged for treason on a large tree next to the road. They said that the Tory sometimes played tricks on folks passing that way.

But the story that scared the young sailor the most was that of old Moll DeGrow. Moll was a witch who once lived on Gully Road and made life miserable for those around her. She soured milk and made dogs turn vicious and caused horses to bolt; she was even accused of causing the death of several infants in the neighborhood. Finally, folks got so scared that they formed a mob and went to burn the witch to death. But when they reached her house, Moll DeGrow was already dead, sitting bolt upright in her chair with a cruel smile on her lifeless face. She was buried in the Mount Prospect Cemetery on Gully Road, and her malicious ghost continued to haunt the place long after her body had turned to dust.

The young sailor stopped and shouted above the storm. "Captain, you're not thinking of going down Gully Road?"

The captain turned and looked at his companion in amazement. "Of course I am, boy!" he shouted. "You ain't scared of ghosts, are you?" He laughed and cursed the ghosts and the storms in such salty language that the young man's ears turned red again.

"Come on," the captain said and stomped onto Gully Road. The young sailor didn't want to look foolish, so he followed, his heart pounding in fear. The rain beat down fiercely and the wind howled around them, making the already dark and shadowy road even more menacing. The captain started singing a boisterous song about a naughty young girl and a sailor to cheer their spirits. But all the young man could think about was Moll DeGrow. He kept whirling around whenever thunder crashed overhead. Each time it happened, the captain cursed loudly and called him a coward.

As they slogged ahead, the young sailor became aware of a twitchy feeling at the nape of his neck—the feeling he always got when someone stared at him. Perhaps they were being followed! He glanced nervously over his shoulder, trying to see who else was out and about on such a foul night. He was half-expecting to encounter the wild-eyed ghost of Moll DeGrow, but instead he saw a dark figure dressed in the clothes of a clergyman. The young sailor relaxed. If they were accompanied on their journey by a man of the cloth, then they had nothing to fear.

Just then the captain started swearing and swatting at the rain, grumbling at the foul weather and the deep mud on the road. Behind them the clergyman chuckled. The young sailor was puzzled by the sound, which was loud enough to hear over the wind and heavy rain. He glanced back and noticed something strange: The clergyman's clothes were completely dry, even though he was walking through the rain without an umbrella or any sort of foul-weather gear. The sailor shivered a bit, pulled his coat closer around him, and tried to hurry the captain past the graveyard and farther away from this odd fellow.

The captain didn't want to be hurried along. He cursed again, louder this time, and the clergyman laughed audibly. As lightning flashed around them, the young sailor looked back at the stranger once more. The man's clothes were steaming slightly, as if the rain were hitting a burning object and instantly evaporating. Stunned, the young sailor grabbed his captain by the arm but managed to drag him only a few feet before the captain stopped dead, cussing and swearing as only a veteran seaman can.

When the clergyman heard this string of expletives, he laughed so long and so gleefully that the old salt finally took notice. The captain and the young sailor turned to confront the man who was following them. In the sudden dazzle of a lightning bolt, they both saw that the fellow's legs ended in cloven hooves, that his forehead sported two small horns, and that his eyes burned with the red fires of hell.

The captain swore again, this time in fright. The stranger continued to laugh, baring pointed teeth that gleamed in the darkness.

"It's the Devil!" shouted the young sailor. He took to his heels and fled at high speed down Gully Road, followed by his captain. When they reached the relative safety of River Road, they paused just long enough to ascertain that they had left the Devil far behind; then they jogged the rest of the way to Bellevue, making the journey home in record time.

They stopped together at the captain's house, which was the closest, and found some comfort in a bottle of whiskey. Then the young sailor staggered to his home on the next street, vowing that he would never set foot on Gully Road again.

GULLY ROAD

The following morning, the captain dropped by to speak to the young man's parents about his wonderful performance aboard the ship and to offer his protégé the position of second mate on his next voyage. The young sailor was ecstatic and accepted the offer without hesitation. His parents, disappointed that he would not join his father in the family store, nonetheless supported this decision and wished their son well in his chosen career.

So the young sailor accompanied his captain back to the ship to help unload the cargo and prepare the schooner for her next voyage. By mutual consent the two men took the long route to the port, thus avoiding Gully Road and the evil spirits that haunted its length. One trip down that road was enough.

29

Just One Sip

ATLANTIC CITY

The casino was hot and noisy that night. My friends were playing the slot machines like there was no tomorrow, but I had already won a tidy sum and didn't want to blow the money on another game of chance. So I decided to pocket the cash and go outside for a walk.

Not many people were on the boardwalk, which was fine by me after the crowded casino. I slipped down to the beach and listened to the soft grumble of ocean waves as I strolled along in the semidarkness that had settled around the glow of the city. I like coming to Atlantic City every once in a while, not so much for the glitz and glitter, but because my family has lived along this section of the Jersey shore for several generations.

On this visit, as always, I thought of the stories my great-grandmother told when my brothers and I were little. To hear granny speak of it, the Jersey shore was littered with ghosts and dark creatures of all kinds. Somewhere to the south, the skeleton of a murdered pirate guarded treasure buried by Captain Kidd. To the north, the spectral form of a black dog with a hatchet wound in its head threatened people walking along a lonely stretch of beach. In life the faithful hound had dragged the body of his drowned master to shore, only to have it desecrated by looters. The evil men killed the hound with a hatchet when it threatened them and made away with the dead sailor's belongings. From that day forward, the ghost of the faithful dog refused to allow anyone near the place where his master's body once lay.

My favorite story was the tale of the phantom ship of Captain Sandovate. According to my granny, Don Sandovate voyaged from Spain to the New World in search of treasure, which he found in abundance. But among his crew were many sailors who did not wish to share this newfound wealth with the monarchs of Spain. On their return journey up the Atlantic coast, the sailors mutinied and imprisoned their captain, tying him to the main mast and refusing to give him food or drink. Day after day, the captain lay exposed to the hot sun, his body drying up as the treacherous sailors worked around him.

Finally, his pride broken, Don Sandovate begged: "Water. Please. Just one sip of water." The mutineers found this amusing and started carrying water up to the main mast and holding it just out of reach of their former captain.

In the terrible heat of the dry summer, the captain did not survive long; he succumbed to exposure and thirst a few days after the mutiny. The new captain, a greedy Spaniard with no compassion in his soul, left Don Sandovate tied to the mast, his body withering away, while the ship turned pirate and plundered its way up the coast. But Providence was watching the ruthless men. A massive storm arose and drove the ship deep into the Atlantic, where it sank with all hands, the body of Don Sandovate still tied to the broken mast.

Shortly after this event a phantom ship appeared along the coast, most often in the calm just before a storm. It looked like a ruined Spanish treasure ship. Observers noticed that its mast was broken, its sails were torn, and the corpse of a noble-looking Spaniard was tied to the main mast. The ship was crewed by hideous skeletons wearing ragged clothing. As the vessel passed other ships or houses near the shore, the skeletons would stretch out bony hands and cry, "Water. Please. Just one sip of water." But no one could help them, for the crew of Don Sandovate was eternally doomed to roam the Atlantic, suffering from thirst in payment for their terrible deeds against the captain and the good people they had plundered.

This scene played through my mind as the sea sighed and lapped at my feet. The wind was picking up and clouds were scuttling over the full moon, obscuring it from sight. *A storm is coming*, I thought, pulling my coat tighter around me.

The wind hissed and crackled around my ears, and in it I could almost hear voices saying, "Water. Just one sip." I shuddered, cursing my vivid imagination. Granny's stories always spooked me, but I felt more frightened than usual. After all, I was walking alone on the same coastline where Sandovate's men had once marauded and killed for the sake of treasure they did not live to enjoy.

It seemed best to head back to the boardwalk and the casinos. But before I could turn around, a flicker of light out at sea caught my eye. Through the growing mist, I looked for a pleasure boat or a late-night fisherman. Instead, I saw a tall ship with ragged sails rapidly approaching the shore. It was a ruined Spanish treasure galleon from days of yore. And to my horrified fascination, it glowed in the dark.

JUST ONE SIP

The wind around me picked up the hiss of voices, which I could now hear clearly. "Water. Please. Just one sip of water." The voices wailed in my ear, and I could see skeletal shapes on deck, stretching their hands toward me. I panicked. With a shout I covered my ears, turned my back on the approaching nightmare, and ran as fast as I could to the boardwalk. Yet the terrible pleas echoed on: "Water. Just one sip of water."

I leapt up the steps and onto the boardwalk as if the Devil himself were chasing me. A strolling couple looked at me strangely and moved to the other side of the boardwalk to avoid me. I whirled around to face the misty sea. It was empty of all save the dim reflection of the well-lit city around me. The breakers murmured against the shore and the wind whispered softly above them, but there were no longer voices in it.

I shook my head, unsure of what I had seen. Had the phantom ship of Don Sandovate really appeared before me, or had I dreamed the whole encounter? I did not know, but the pounding of my heart and the shaking of my hands convinced me that whatever had happened, I did not want it to happen again.

As I hurried back into the glitz and glitter of the crowded casino, I decided that I had enjoyed one too many visits to the Jersey shore. Next year, I was going to Las Vegas.

30

Death of a Wizard

I heard a happy squeal from the far side of the porch, and my one-year-old son said, "Kitty cat!" I sighed, set aside the string beans I was snapping, and rose to my feet. Yes, there was Stick, sashaying its way across the floorboards. Timmy was in hot pursuit, crawling as fast as he could and trying to grab the bottom of the ornate walking stick as it floated over to me.

"Good afternoon, Stick," I said as it swept me a polite bow. "What does Uncle Jerry want now?"

The magic walking stick bent toward me, and I removed the note attached to it with a piece of string. On the note was a list of items Uncle Jerry needed from the blacksmith. It was no surprise that Uncle Jerry knew that my husband—Timothy—was going into town. After all, my uncle was a wizard. Long before I was born, he sold his soul to the Devil in exchange for magical powers.

I actually met the Devil once when he paid a call on Uncle Jerry. He was a tall man, dark and handsome in a wicked sort of way, with sharp red-brown eyes and a pointed beard. He very politely took off his hat when I was introduced to him, revealing two small horns on the top of his head; I also saw a tail poking out of the back of his suit. I was more fascinated than alarmed by "Mr. Satan," as I called him. The Devil chuckled and patted me on the head before sending me to see my aunt in the kitchen while he talked with my uncle.

Once I removed the note, Stick began a solemn waltz across the porch, staying just out of reach of my frantically crawling son. It was a game they played whenever Stick came to my house. But on this day I grew alarmed as Timmy headed straight for the edge of the porch. Dropping the note and leaping toward the baby, I shouted at Stick in a reproving manner: "You know better! You are supposed to protect Timmy, not lure him into danger."

It was technically not possible for a walking stick to express indignation, but somehow Stick managed it. It demonstrated its ability to block off the edge of the porch so the baby would not tumble over the side.

"All right, I apologize," I said.

Stick bobbed up and down to indicate that it accepted my apology. Stick had often watched over me when I was a small child, and it was not above reminding me of that fact.

"Bear with me, Stick," I said. "I am still new to motherhood."

Stick radiated understanding.

"Will you watch Timmy while I take this note to his father?" I asked. Stick bobbed up and down again in agreement and began hustling the baby toward the door.

I took the note down to the stables, where Timothy was hitching up the horse. He was a brawny man with fair hair and brown eyes, and I loved him madly.

"Uncle Jerry's list?" he asked, anticipating my request. I laughed and handed it to him. Not just any man would be willing to marry into a family with a known wizard, but Timothy had joined us gladly. His compassion, understanding, and wry sense of humor exactly matched that of my uncle, who had heartily approved the match.

I returned to the house and Stick headed out the door, leaving a distraught little boy behind him. I picked up the baby and followed Stick to the front lawn.

"Tell Uncle Jerry we could use some firewood," I called as Stick floated down the lane toward my uncle's farm. "There are a couple of oaks at the edge of the property that will do the trick." I gestured toward them with my free hand, and Timmy tried to grab my fingers.

Before I finished speaking, there came a report like the crack of rifle fire, and two towering oaks fell down in the field by the house, neatly avoiding the fence. A moment later an axe made its way out of the toolshed.

"Thank you!" I called after Stick.

By the time supper was on the table, both wood boxes were filled and the rest of the wood was piling itself neatly at the corner of the house. Timothy came in with the parcels from town. He dropped a kiss on my cheek as he set them down.

"I stopped at Uncle Jerry's place for a moment to drop off the items on his list," he told me. "Your aunt sent over a pie." He laid it down on the counter and proceeded to say grace. Then he looked at me gravely and delivered unexpected news: "Uncle Jerry is not doing well. Aunt had the doctor over again. He doesn't think your uncle will live out the week."

I slowly put down my fork, trying to take in his words. I could not imagine life without Uncle Jerry. "He's sure?" I asked.

"The doctor is sure, Aunt is sure, and so is Uncle Jerry," said Timothy, taking my hand. "I am sorry, Isabelle." I squeezed his hand tightly, grateful that he was there to comfort me.

Moments later the baby dumped his entire plate onto the floor, grinned at both of us, and said, "Uh-oh!" We laughed, the sorrow eased for a moment, and I hurried to wet some rags and clean up the mess.

I couldn't sleep that night, and so I went softly to the porch—careful not to wake my sleeping men—and sat watching the stars and thinking about Uncle Jerry. He was quite a character. As a young man he took a job working for the Jones family in Hanover Furnace. The family had some kind of disagreement with my uncle, however, and refused to pay his wages. So Uncle Jerry used his wizardry to stop their furnaces from burning. The whole site closed down for several days, at which point Uncle Jerry offered to fix the problem in exchange for his back pay. As soon as the Joneses agreed, a blast of freezing air flooded the site and a flock of snow-white crows flew out of the chimneys. Then the furnaces burst into flames. The Joneses hurriedly counted out Uncle Jerry's money, completely spooked by this strange display of power.

You would think the Joneses had learned their lesson, but a few years later they had another disagreement with my uncle and again refused to pay his wages. This time, Uncle Jerry sent their team of horses bolting into the pond. He relented after the money was counted, levitating the soggy team out of the water and transporting horses and carriage to the nearest hitching post. After that the Joneses paid Uncle Jerry right on time.

My uncle used his supernatural powers carefully. Those men who cheated and lied and stole from the good people in our community found their cows straying into swamps, their gold coins turning into clamshells, their meat spoiling, or their dairy products going sour. The wholesome, upright folks were given assistance when someone got sick or their crops failed.

But my uncle had a quirky side, too—he was very fond of practical jokes. Sometimes the wind would whip around a local's cottage and whisper that person's name. Other times Uncle Jerry would hitch a tiny rooster to his carriage and drive it into town. And he loved to send Stick on errands. The owner of the neighborhood tavern grew resigned to the sight of Stick sashaying into his bar, looking for a bottle of whiskey to take home to my uncle.

I chuckled softly and wiped away tears, my head full of memories. The front door creaked open and Timothy came tiptoeing outside. He sat beside me on the porch swing and put his arm around my shoulders. We cuddled, listening to the still sounds of the night until at last I fell asleep in his arms.

We watched and waited for two days. I spent as much time as I could with my uncle, reading to him from his favorite books and talking over old times. I was very worried about his contract with the Devil, and I told him so frankly as we watched Timmy playing with blocks on the bedroom floor.

"Don't worry, Isabelle," Uncle Jerry said with a feeble wink. "There's more than one way to outwit the Devil." Stick, who was hovering near the doorway, bobbed up and down in agreement.

At that moment Timmy heaved his bottom up in the air, braced himself, and stood upright for the very first time. When he was confident of his balance, the baby looked up at us with a big smile and clapped his hands. Uncle Jerry and I cheered, and Stick pounded its tip into the floor in applause. Aunt came running upstairs to see what all the fuss was about; Timmy managed to wave to her before falling down. It was a wonderful moment.

A little before eleven o'clock that night, Stick knocked on our bedroom window. We came awake at once, and Timothy let Stick in. We knew even before we read the note that Uncle Jerry was dying. "Take the baby with you to their house," Timothy instructed me. "I will go fetch the doctor."

I wrapped Timmy up in my shawl and practically ran down the lane to my uncle's house. Aunt opened the door. It was obvious that she had been weeping.

"Is he . . ." I started to ask.

"I'm still here," Uncle Jerry called from upstairs. "Come up and say good-bye, my dear."

I carried the baby upstairs and placed him next to the pale form of my beloved uncle. Jerry hugged Timmy and then touched his wrinkled hand to my cheek. "I love you, my dear. You have been the best of nieces and a good chum. Tell Timothy to take good care of my little girl and this baby of yours."

I bent down and kissed his cheek, holding back the tears as best I could since he couldn't abide "maudlin sentimentality."

"I love you, too, Uncle," I said. "Try not to let the Devil take your soul."

"Oh, he's coming for me, no doubt," Uncle Jerry replied. "But your old uncle still has a trick or two up his sleeve. Now shoo!"

Wiping away a few tears that had escaped down my cheeks, I picked up the baby, studied my uncle's face one last time, and went to the kitchen to sit with my aunt, who was preparing a cup of tea.

There came a knock on the front door.

"That must be Timothy with the doctor," my aunt said, rising. I heard her unlatch the door and then shriek. The man on the other side was tall and dark and handsome in a wicked sort of way, with sharp red-brown eyes and a pointed beard. He very politely took off his hat, revealing two small horns on the top of his head. A tail poked out of the back of his suit. It was the Devil.

"I have come for Jerry, if you please," he said, bowing to my aunt. She gaped at him.

"J-J-Just a moment," she finally stammered. "I'll see if he's ready. Isabelle will entertain you in the parlor." And with that she fled up the stairs.

Isabelle will entertain you in the parlor? I thought in alarm, hitching Timmy a little higher up on my hip. But aloud I was as polite as ever. "Won't you come in?" I asked, holding the door for him. The Devil entered, and I took his fancy hat and coat from him.

"The parlor is this way," I said, leading the Devil to that room. I put Timmy on the floor and he promptly crawled away to look at the wood box. "Please take a seat," I added.

The Devil sat on the sofa, and I took a chair opposite him. "My, how you've grown, Isabelle," the Devil exclaimed once I was seated. "You are quite the elegant young woman now. And this is your son?"

"Yes, this is Timmy," I answered, gesturing to my son, who was trying to stuff a piece of kindling in his mouth. When he heard his name, Timmy dropped the wood and crawled over to us. He sat up and regarded the Devil for a moment.

"Kitty cat!" he said suddenly, pointing to the Devil's tail.

I was deeply mortified. Snatching up my son, I said, "I am *so* sorry! He calls everyone kitty cat."

"Not to worry, my dear girl. I am flattered," the Devil said with a charming smile. "He is an intelligent lad. I suppose you've had him baptized?"

"Yes, we have," I replied quickly as Timmy struggled against me, wanting to get back down on the floor. "We felt that one wizard in the family was enough." I put the baby down, and he crawled to the center of the room and sat staring at the Devil in fascination.

"Too bad," said the Devil.

The sound of raised voices came from the floor above us. "I understand about the contract for your soul!" shouted my aunt. "But does he have to come *here* to collect you? What will the neighbors say?"

"Surely he dressed nicely for the occasion," Uncle Jerry said in his most placating voice.

"That's not the point!" my aunt roared. "I am a churchgoing woman and have a reputation to maintain in this community."

I smiled awkwardly and pretended not to hear the argument raging above us.

"How are things in Hades these days?" I asked pleasantly.

"Hotter than the blazes," the Devil said.

"So I understand," I said. "Earth must be a pleasant change for you."

"Yes, indeed," the Devil replied. Then he changed the subject. "So tell me, has young Timmy learned to walk yet?"

"He's trying," I said. "Timmy, show Mr. Satan how you stand up."

Obediently, Timmy crouched on all fours. He stuck his little bottom into the air, braced himself, and then unfolded upward with a frown of concentration that turned into a broad smile when he gained his balance.

"Bravo!" cried the Devil, clapping his hands. Timmy laughed excitedly and clapped hands, too. The movement upset his delicate balance, sending him to the floor again.

At that moment my aunt entered the parlor and the Devil rose politely. "My husband will see you now," she said nervously, twisting her hands. "We've said our good-byes."

"Thank you, madam," he said gravely and turned toward me. "Farewell, Isabelle."

"Good-bye, Mr. Satan," I said, curtseying politely. "It was a pleasure meeting you again."

"Really?" asked the Devil in genuine amusement. "Most people don't think so. Take care, my dear. I am afraid I probably won't be seeing you again. Unless you'd care to make a little contract?"

"No, thank you," I replied. "It's kind of you to ask, but I blister if I stay in the heat too long."

"We can't have that," the Devil said. He gave Timmy a merry grin, and the baby waved bye-bye to the "kitty cat." Then the Devil went upstairs to collect my Uncle Jerry.

By the time Timothy arrived with the doctor, the Devil was gone and Uncle Jerry was dead. Stick lay lifelessly beside him on the bed. My aunt crouched beside Uncle Jerry's still form and whispered, "I didn't really mean what I said about the neighbors." She stroked his hand tenderly.

"He knew that," I assured her, touching her shoulder. She stood up, and I took her into my arms.

My husband was a tower of strength over the next few days, arranging for a simple funeral (without a minister) and then bringing my aunt to stay with us until the first empty days had passed and she was ready to go home.

I missed Stick almost as much as I missed my uncle. Stick usually appeared at our house two or three times a day, but now it sat motionless in the corner of our kitchen. Little Timmy kept prodding it, trying to get it to play with him, but Stick had died with my uncle.

I was sitting in my favorite chair on the porch about a month after Uncle Jerry's death, snapping more green beans for our Sunday dinner, when my son cried, "Kitty cat!" He pushed up his bottom, stood upright, and staggered proudly across the floor of the porch, his little arms stretched toward Stick, who was hovering in the doorway. I gasped and dropped the bowl of green beans, spilling them everywhere.

"Stick!" I cried, tears of joy streaming down my face.

Stick started shuffling across the floor of the porch with the funny dance he always did for my son. Timmy was still not too steady on his feet. He sat down and pursued Stick at his fastest crawl, repeating "Kitty cat!" over and over again.

I rose, brushing the green beans off my skirt. "Stick?" I called again in a quavering voice.

"I'm here, too, my dear," said Uncle Jerry. He materialized beside Stick and bowed first to me, then to my son. Then my uncle and Stick waltzed down the length of the porch, much to the delight of Timmy.

"You came back as a ghost?" I asked, stunned.

DEATH OF A WIZARD

Uncle Jerry turned with a flourish. "There's more than one way to outwit the Devil, my dear," he said with a wink. "Now I must see your aunt. Come, Stick."

I picked up baby Timmy, and we both waved as my semitransparent uncle and Stick walked down the lane toward home.

31

Stolen Gold

RED OAK GROVE

Bill Mullen looked furtively left and right, but no one was approaching. He did not care to be seen so close to Peggy Clevenger's place—not on this night. Her daughter and son-in-law had taken the wagon and gone to town, and Peggy had not been seen or heard from all day. Bill thought she had probably turned herself into a rabbit, as was her usual practice, so that she could spend the evening spying on the good folks in town. Wherever Peggy was, at the moment her house stood empty in the twilight, full of the witch's stolen gold.

Bill darted across the dusty road in the twilight and hid among the shadows on the far side. As he slipped closer to his goal, he debated with his conscience. Everyone knew that Peggy Clevenger was a witch. She had put a curse on old Thomas after he sold her some bad fish. Violently ill and close to death, Thomas had dragged himself from his bed, drawn a likeness of the harridan on a piece of wood, and shot at it with a silver bullet. He missed the heart of the witch in the drawing but pierced the right hand. At once old Thomas felt better. The very next day Peggy Clevenger appeared with a bandage wrapped around her right hand. She told everyone that her dog had bitten her, but old Thomas knew otherwise.

It was not wrong to steal from a witch, Bill told himself. Peggy Clevenger was responsible for much of the bad luck that plagued the area: Cows went dry, horses threw their shoes, winter came too early and stayed too long, crops failed—all because of the witch-woman.

It was not fair that this same woman was also the proprietress of a very successful business. The Half-Way Place was a popular stop along the road through Red Oak Grove; the Clevenger family sold good, hot food for reasonable prices and kept the hotel as tidy as a pin.

Bill, on the other hand, had endured nothing but hardship from the moment he first set foot in Red Oak Grove. His crops had failed two years in a row, his wife had left him for a traveling salesman, and he'd had to shoot his favorite horse when it broke its leg after being spooked by a rabbit in front of Half-Way Place. Bill was sure the rabbit was Peggy Clevenger in disguise. He had openly criticized the witch more than once, and that was her revenge.

Following the death of his horse, Bill started a whisper campaign against the witch and managed to persuade some of her more susceptible customers to take their business elsewhere. His triumph was short-lived, however, for his little daughter— his only child—took ill with fever and died in a single night. Bill knew that this was no accident; this was the work of a witch, and he knew which witch it was. He was furious and kept trying to come up with a way to wreak vengeance upon Peggy Clevenger.

Then Bill was given notice that his mortgage was being called in. If he did not pay up immediately, he was going to lose

STOLEN GOLD

his house and land. Bill was certain that Peggy had a hand in this matter, too, though he was not sure how she had managed it.

The only recourse he had, Bill told himself as he wriggled in through the kitchen window, was to take Peggy's stolen gold. In the process he would avenge himself on the woman who had turned the affections of his wife from him and taken the life of his precious daughter. With a tiny smile, he picked up the axe resting beside the wood box and hefted it over his shoulder. Then he began searching the house.

Bill looked high and low but found nothing. Desperate to locate the object of his desire before anyone returned, he began ripping apart cushions, overturning furniture, and chopping up floorboards with his axe. There was no gold; not even a single copper penny came to light. In despair and rage, Bill made his way back to the kitchen. Maybe the money was in the root cellar.

"Just what do you think you are up to, Bill Mullen?" a woman's voice demanded. Bill whirled to find Peggy Clevenger standing in the doorway that led to the garden. She held a bundle of freshly picked herbs in one hand and a lantern in the other. "You should knock before entering the home of a respectable person," she said, laying down her things and removing her cloak and hat.

"You are hardly respectable, you old witch," Bill said.

At that moment Peggy noticed the disarray in her normally neat kitchen.

"What is going on here?" she asked icily, glaring at her neighbor.

"Where is the gold you stole, you worshipper of Satan?" Bill shouted, anger and frustration overwhelming him. "Tell me now, or I will rip you apart with this axe and free the world of your sinful presence."

"Gold? I do not have any gold," Peggy said. "And I am not a witch. You shouldn't listen to false rumors, Bill."

"You lie," said Bill, turning red with rage. "You are a liar and a thief. You turned my wife against me, and you took the life of my daughter."

Peggy backed away from her wild-eyed neighbor, who shrieked "Give me the gold!" and then ran at her, swinging the axe. Peggy screamed and tried to flee, but her back was against the wall. With one terrible blow Bill felled the alleged witch, and with a second he took off her head.

Gasping, Bill stared down at Peggy's bloodstained, headless body, suddenly realizing what he had done. His neighbors might not care that he had murdered a witch, but the local magistrate would have other ideas. Grabbing the lantern, Bill set fire to the kitchen and then the parlor. Then he ducked out of the house, slid into the shadows, and disposed of the axe in the nearest pond.

As Peggy's house blazed behind him, Bill crept furtively home. He heard the Clevenger's daughter and her husband shouting from down the lane, and the rattle of their wagon drummed into his ears as they sped by parallel to his path. He did not join the fire brigade or the milling neighbors until he had cleaned the blood from his hands and face and had burned his gory clothing.

By daylight the Clevenger house had burnt clear down to the ground. In the aftermath the townsfolk realized that there was no sign of any gold among the ruins. Then Peggy's headless body was discovered, and her daughter and son-in-law came under suspicion. Many people reckoned that they had stolen the gold, killed Peggy, and set up a timed device that would ignite the house while they were away. No one had any proof to support this accusation, however, so no arrests were made.

Bill managed to borrow enough money from a friend to help stave off his creditors, and his luck changed for the better after the fire. But his conscience would not give him any peace. Night after night he dreamt of Peggy Clevenger, reliving the murder scene just prior to the fire.

Soon rumors of a headless woman seen roaming the Pinelands at night came to Bill's ears. People claimed it was Peggy's ghost, searching for her stolen gold. These stories made Bill sick to his stomach; he saw nothing but the witch's face every time he closed his eyes.

One night, as Bill rode home on his horse, he spied a rabbit sitting in the center of the road, starting at him unwaveringly. Bill remembered that Peggy Clevenger had allegedly taken on the appearance of a rabbit when she was alive. He reigned in his horse and shouted savagely at the little creature. It glared at him in the moonlight for another moment and then scampered away. Bill was shaken to the core. The next morning he felt so ill that he could not get out of bed.

Bill grew sicker and sicker, suffering so much that soon he wanted to die. The doctor could find nothing physically wrong with him and finally turned the matter over to the minister. The clergyman urged Bill to confess whatever terrible secret was making him so ill, but the patient only shook his head and claimed that he had no secret. As he denied the truth, Bill heard a quiet chuckle coming from the corner of the room. The headless figure of a woman appeared beside the window. She was wearing the same dress Peggy Clevenger had worn when he murdered her, and her head was tucked under one arm.

"Gold?" whispered the head, sneering at him from underneath the ghost's shoulder. "I do not have any gold."

Bill screamed and sat straight up in bed. "I did it!" he shouted. "I murdered Peggy Clevenger. I was looking for her stolen gold, but I couldn't find it." Bill's face turned bright red and he gasped, clutching his arm as pain thundered through his whole body. He felt heavy and tired. Darkness clouded his vision, and he heard the ghost of Peggy Clevenger whisper, "You shouldn't listen to false rumors, Bill."

With a final cry of remorse, Bill fell lifeless on the bed.

32

Dem Bones

SANDY HOOK

Sandy Hook looks a lot different now than it did in my many-times-great granny's day, when Captain Kidd roamed these waters, stealing gold and burying treasure. According to the story my granny heard when she was a child, the pirate planted a cache of treasure—worth 10,000 British pounds—on Gardiner's Island. Then, knowing the law was on his trail, he traveled up the Jersey coast looking for the perfect spot to bury the bulk of his wealth; he had gained much of it by capturing the *Quedah Merchant*, an Indian ship filled with gold and spices, silk and guns, and enough treasures to make the heart of any pirate merry.

Captain Kidd found the perfect place near a grove of gnarled, windswept pines on Sandy Hook. One moonless night, the *Adventure Galley* slid silently into harbor. Before the astounded eyes of two hidden watchers, a crew of scurvy buccaneers armed with cutlasses and pistols rowed boatload after boatload of heavy chests to the shore. They were accompanied by a tall, proud man with red whiskers and a cocked hat—Kidd, of course. His men eventually disappeared into the grove with the chests, and there they remained for a very long time—long enough, according to the secret observers, to bury a vast amount of treasure. Just before dawn they emerged from the trees, rowed back to the *Adventure Galley*, and sailed away into the last vestiges of the dark night.

The eager witnesses kept this information quiet. Two days later they scurried down to the pine grove, armed with lanterns and shovels. But nary a gold coin found they. In frustration, they shared their tale with a few other men in the region, who helped them search. Soon the story spread even farther, and night after night the pine grove was host to a new group of seekers. A few decades of random digging destroyed the grove; by my granny's time there was nothing left save a few stunted trees, some matted grass, and on certain dark nights, Dem Bones.

Dem Bones are the skeletal crew of Captain Kidd. According to my granny, they sail up the coast in a ship made of shadows. This vessel anchors near the shores of Sandy Hook, and two or three boats are lowered from her side, filled with glowing skeletons wearing cocked hats and tattered buccaneers' garb. Around their waists are belts full of pistols and long cutlasses. The biggest of Dem Bones—probably the first mate—has a skeletal parrot perched on his shoulder.

Dem Bones carry heavy trunks full of treasure onto the shore and set them down where the pine grove once stood. Then the crew hauls out kegs and kegs of whiskey, and one of the skeletons takes out a fiddle. A phantom fire is lit on the sand, and Dem Bones start to sing and dance so rowdily that the noise would wake the dead—if they weren't already awake. When they are exhausted, the glowing figures collapse on the sand and tell stories about the ships they have captured and the treasure

DEM BONES

they have amassed. Some of Dem Bones open the chests and take out jewels and ropes of pearls to adorn themselves. Others toss gold coins back and forth as if they were a child's ball. Just before dawn Dem Bones pack up the treasure and return to the ship of shadows. One by one, the skeletons disappear into the hold; then the ship draws anchor and sails away.

I'd heard the tales of Dem Bones all my life and wondered if they were true. So one dark night when there was no moon, I slipped away from home and drove to Sandy Hook. I parked my car in a safe spot and hiked out to the former pine grove, eventually settling down with a snack behind a gnarled old bush that looked as if it had been there since Captain Kidd arrived with his treasure. It was a warm summer night. Between the food and the sweet-smelling ocean breeze tinged with salt, I was lulled to sleep.

The sharp shriek of a parrot calling "Captain Kidd! Captain Kidd!" woke me, how many hours later I do not know. I sat up in astonishment, knocking my head on the low branches of the bush. The night was alive with an eerie, greenish light and the murmur of happy, drunken voices. I peered toward the commotion and saw a crew of rowdy skeletons dressed in the clothes of ancient buccaneers. They were seated around a fire, passing a large keg from hand to hand and drinking deeply from it. The whiskey passed right through their bones and spilled onto the sandy ground, but this bothered them not a whit. The skeleton of the parrot was on the ground near the fire. It pecked intently at a dark patch and then squawked indignantly.

"Give us a song, matey!" shouted a skeleton that was casually cleaning a gleaming pistol. He pointed it at another skeleton that was tuning a fiddle balanced on its bony knees.

The fiddler gave him a toothy grin and began to play a cheerful sea shanty that made all the dead pirates sing.

My heart was racing with such a combination of delight and sheer terror that I didn't know what to do. It was Dem Bones! All of my granny's stories were true.

A couple of Dem Bones got up and started dancing, the rattle and clatter of their frames creating a countermelody to the fiddle tune. When the song mentioned treasure, the first mate opened a large chest and flung gold and silver coins to the other members of the crew. A giant skeleton draped itself in ropes of pearls and loaded every finger with rings. Then it performed the Highland Fling for the amusement of its companions.

One gold coin sailed right over the bush, landed on my shoulder with a soft thump, and slipped onto the sand. I picked it up and examined it. It felt solid and looked authentic. I bit down on the coin and got a sour, metallic taste on my tongue. My eyes widened in wonder. It was a real gold doubloon! With trembling hands, I slipped it into my pocket.

An excited shout came from one of Dem Bones near the shore. Then all the pirates gave a loud cheer as a boat slid to a halt in the sand and a tall, swaggering ghost with red whiskers and a cocked hat stepped ashore. It was Captain Kidd. The parrot started squawking and flapping its skeletal wings, making such a racket that no one could hear a word the captain said. Kidd picked it up and put it on his shoulder, where it bobbed its skeleton head up and down contentedly and bit the captain's ear.

Kidd was making his way toward the fire when suddenly he stopped. "Men, we are not alone!" he cried, drawing his pistol. I froze and my skin prickled with goose bumps. Dem

Bones gave an outraged shout, whirled around, and drew their cutlasses.

Captain Kidd pointed right at the bush where I was hidden. "There's a stranger in our midst! Get him, mateys!"

I leapt up and started running for my car, which was hidden several miles away. Dem Bones gave another shout and pursued me. Anyone who has ever been chased down a beach in the middle of the night by a band of pirate skeletons will understand the absolute terror—combined with a slight sense of absurdity— that I felt at that moment. I thought my heart would burst out of my chest, but I didn't dare slow down. Dem Bones rattled and clattered behind me, and from far off, the parrot continued to call "Captain Kidd! Captain Kidd!"

I suppose they only meant to frighten me off—a task they accomplished successfully, I might add—as the sounds of pursuit ceased after about five minutes. I kept running until I reached my car, however, and then drove like the dickens until a highway patrolman stopped me for speeding. Doubtful that my explanation would impress the officer (except maybe to convince him that I had been drinking), I accepted the ticket without protest.

Pure relief flooded over me when I finally made it home. In the light of the next morning, I was inclined to believe that the whole incident had been a dream. At least, that was my theory until I picked up my jeans and something fell out of a pocket and rolled under the bed. Curious, I got down on my hands and knees and felt around in the dust until my hand closed over something round and firm and cool to the touch—a gold doubloon from a pirate's buried treasure.

33

The Treasure Trove

SCHOOLEY'S MOUNTAIN

The year was 1788. The new Mistress Smith and I had just purchased a plot of land on Schugl's Hill and built our first home. I was working as the local blacksmith, so I was always the first in town to hear the latest news. My pretty wife, who went to town only once a fortnight to shop, had to make do with retellings from me. One night I came home with a particularly enticing piece of gossip.

"Pirate's gold?" Priscilla asked in astonishment when I told her the rumor that was buzzing around town. "Buried on top of the mountain?"

"That's what folks are saying," I told her. "They swear it's the truth. The only trouble is, a scurvy lot of pirates was murdered and buried along with the treasure, and their ghosts chase away anyone who tries to find it."

Priscilla shivered. "I believe it," she said, rubbing her hands nervously as she stared out into the late-autumn night. The howl of the wind against our house, the creaking of tree branches as they rubbed against each another, the shadows that crisscrossed our yard as clouds scuttled across the moon—all of these things had turned our happy home into a place where ghosts might tread, if the conditions were right. The whole of Schugl's Hill was covered with the sort of thick forests and strange creatures that made walking at night a fearful undertaking.

"There's a fellow in town, name of Rogers, who has successfully banished ghosts in the past in similar circumstances," I said. "He's an educated fellow, used to teach school up in Connecticut. He learned how to reason with dangerous spirits from some old texts brought to America from the Orient—so maybe he can help us. They are holding a town meeting tonight to vote on what we should do about the treasure. Would you like to go?"

Priscilla's face lit up. "Oh, yes," she said. She changed into her town clothes while I hitched up the wagon.

So many families gathered for the meeting that we had to hold it in the church. There was a great debate regarding the size of the treasure, how it would be split up, and the best way to deal with those who guarded it. Ransford Rogers came forward to speak on this last matter. After being introduced, he presented his credentials, which were even more impressive than I had realized. Then he offered to commune with the spirit world to assess the situation on top of the mountain. A few moments after Rogers went into a trance, several terrible, loud blasts sounded outside, and twinkling lights shot upward into the sky before cascading down. Everyone rushed to the windows to watch.

"The evil spirits have spoken!" Rogers shouted above the hubbub. "They guard the treasure buried at the top of the mountain, and they must be appeased—or the treasure trove cannot be removed."

The sounds and lights ceased as abruptly as they appeared, and the townsfolk were persuaded to take their seats. "What must we do to appease the spirits?" the owner of the sawmill asked.

Rogers said that he would ask the spirits to use him as a medium and then write their answer to this question down on paper. He had learned this technique from an old sailor who had learned it from an ancient holy man in the Orient.

Rogers started chanting softly in a foreign tongue and slowly closed his eyes. Everyone in the room watched him in silence. I held my breath, not wanting to disturb him at a critical moment. Suddenly the schoolteacher went rigid. He dipped his pen into the inkpot and began to write. Over his shoulder, the owner of the mercantile read the words aloud. The gist of the message was simple: The spirits wanted cash paid to the man with whom they communicated. If the townsfolk were generous to their new friend, then the spirits would be generous to us. Twelve pounds silver was the sum they required from each family that desired a stake in the treasure.

Priscilla glanced sharply at me. Twelve pounds was a lot of money for a young couple just starting out. It was up to her to decide. I wanted to find the treasure as much as the next man, but keeping my wife happy was the most important thing to me. Finally, she nodded.

Forty families decided to participate in the treasure hunt. The next day, Rogers collected his money. Even the sheriff and the town grocer—a stingy man by all accounts—paid up. I shook my head when I did the math. Four hundred and eighty pounds was a small fortune. I only hoped that the treasure would be worth the price we had paid. Still, Rogers seemed trustworthy, and his knowledge of Oriental magic was unparalleled.

Rogers spent the next several days climbing up and down the mountain. I saw him on my way to and from the forge, chanting to himself, examining strangely shaped stones, or just

THE TREASURE TROVE

staring at the sky. Whenever he passed, folks would stop what they were doing to watch him.

Finally he approached the prominent local men who were gathered in my smithy discussing the treasure. The spirits, he told them gravely, were still suspicious and needed placating. The upshot was that Rogers needed another twelve pounds from those people who desired a larger stake in the treasure. They would get double the portion of gold from the grateful spirits, who would lead them to the places where the most expensive jewelry and the largest number of coins were deposited.

I reviewed the situation carefully, but no matter how I added and subtracted, another twelve pounds was beyond my means. I reluctantly turned down the offer, but several men took Rogers up on his proposition, the lure of all that gold calling irresistibly to them. Later, when I was closing the smithy for the night, I realized that Rogers had presented his demand for more money when the sheriff was not around. That made me wonder a little. The sheriff was one of the most important men in town. Why hadn't Rogers included him in the new offer?

I had barely reached home when my neighbor came thundering into my yard on a sweaty horse. "The sheriff just arrested Rogers!" he shouted. "He's a fraud!"

Apparently, the grocer's wife had discovered her husband searching their house for any spare cash so that he could participate in Rogers's new scheme. Being an intelligent woman, as well as thrifty, she immediately notified the sheriff. When the sheriff approached Rogers about the matter, the schoolteacher—if he ever was one—tried to run. But the sheriff caught and arrested him.

"What about our money?" Priscilla asked breathlessly. "Did the sheriff get our money back?" The neighbor shook his head.

Rogers did not have the money on him, and so far the sheriff had not been able to make him talk.

As our neighbor departed to spread the news farther, I hitched up the wagon. Then Pricilla and I drove to town to talk to the sheriff about our money. When we reached the main street, we were instantly surrounded by people brimming with the latest report: Rogers had escaped. The sheriff and several local men were in pursuit, and we were confident that the scoundrel would soon be apprehended.

We stayed in town late, hoping for more news, but when it came it was bad. Rogers had slipped away with all of our money. We found out later that the explosions and lights he had claimed were evil spirits actually were fireworks that he had rigged just before coming forward in the town meeting.

"That's the last time I trust a schoolteacher," I told Priscilla. "Especially one that claims to have special Oriental knowledge." She agreed.

It was a long and weary ride home. Still, I couldn't help but think about the rumors of a buried treasure trove. Priscilla soon asked the question on both of our minds: "Do you think there really is pirate's treasure somewhere on this mountain?"

"I honestly don't know what to think," I replied. "If there is, we'll never find it now. Although that probably won't stop some folks from digging!"

Sure enough, just about every inch of dirt on the mountaintop was overturned in the months that followed—but not one gold coin was ever found. As for Ransford Rogers, he was never seen again.

34

Rival Witches

Folks in the Ramapo Mountains were afeared of Handsome Abby and Black Mag, and for good reason: They were two of the most wicked witches in New Jersey, and the rivalry between them was fierce.

Handsome Abby lived in a rundown cottage in the woods. She dressed in rags and had wild hair, buck teeth, bulging brown eyes, and more warts than a toad. She sold herbal remedies from her back door, and whenever little children saw her, they threw stones and ran away.

Black Mag lived alone in a fancy house in town. She was tall and had a terrible beauty that enslaved men. Her long black hair, when unbound, hung to her feet, and her eyes were the blue of the sky before a storm. Her smile was very sweet—and very cruel—and she ran the local mercantile with ruthless efficiency.

When a rival merchant opened a dry-goods store in town, Black Mag bore it with surprising good will, until he began undercutting her prices. Then she set a curse upon him. Dark, shadowy figures would follow him home and call unspeakable things to him from the trees beside his house. His cows died off, one by one, until he had to buy milk and butter from a neighbor.

Many of his special orders failed to arrive. His suppliers were afraid to make the journey to town because their horses were often spooked by strange creatures that came leaping out of the woods. It looked as if the man would be driven out of business.

Then Handsome Abby stepped in. The wife of the dry-goods merchant was a frequent customer of hers, coming weekly to the cottage in the woods to buy herbal remedies for an invalid son. Handsome Abby did not want to lose this prosperous customer, so she set a countercurse upon her rival witch. The next day, Black Mag found dry rot in the boards of her mercantile floor. Then rats got into the shop and ate her inventory. One morning, she opened the door to the mercantile and found an infestation of spiders busily spinning everywhere. Black Mag was furious. She shut the mercantile and stalked home in a rage. Everyone who saw her in the street that day avoided her eye and scurried away as fast as they dared.

In her workroom Black Mag drew upon the powers of darkness and called forth a terrible creature—half-wolf and half-demon—to slay Handsome Abby. Thunder clouds descended upon the town, and lightning struck again and again. Horrible, unearthly voices howled around and around Black Mag's house, screeching wordlessly. The good people in town locked themselves inside their houses, huddled underneath their bedclothes, and prayed to God for protection from the wicked witch.

Handsome Abby knew she had gone too far. Her power did not match that of her rival, and death in the form of a werewolf would soon stalk her. But she was determined that Black Mag would also die. She prepared a secret potion, deep in her woodland cottage—a potion involving roots and berries and a certain poison.

Everyone knew that Black Mag used a special cream on her face to keep it young and beautiful. When Handsome Abby mixed up her potion, she made it resemble this very cream, down to the bottle in which it was contained. Then she sent her familiar—a large black raven—to carry the potion to the home of Black Mag and leave it on the dressing table in her bedroom. Handsome Abby finished just in time; a moment later, she heard the first eerie howl from the hillside and knew that the werewolf had her scent.

The old witch had nowhere to run, and hiding was useless. Even if she climbed a tree, the werewolf would wait beneath it until she grew sleepy and fell from its branches. Grimly, Handsome Abby took out her knife and sat down at the kitchen table, waiting for death. She was determined that the creature would know fear before it finished with her.

The next morning, a farmer seeking a remedy for his sore tooth found Handsome Abby lying dead in her doorway. Her throat had been ripped out by a wolf, and a bloody knife was in her hand. The farmer saw wolf tracks leading away; clutching his rifle, he followed them deep into the woods, determined to kill the creature before it took another life. But the trail disappeared suddenly, as if the wolf had vanished into thin air. The farmer shivered when he saw this. He knew then that the creature had been a werewolf, one summoned specifically to kill the old witch. The farmer was fairly certain that he knew who had brought the creature to life.

When the news of Handsome Abby's death reached town, Black Mag smiled with triumph, opened her newly refurbished mercantile, and discounted all the black fabric she had in stock. The owner of the dry-goods store blanched. While Black Mag

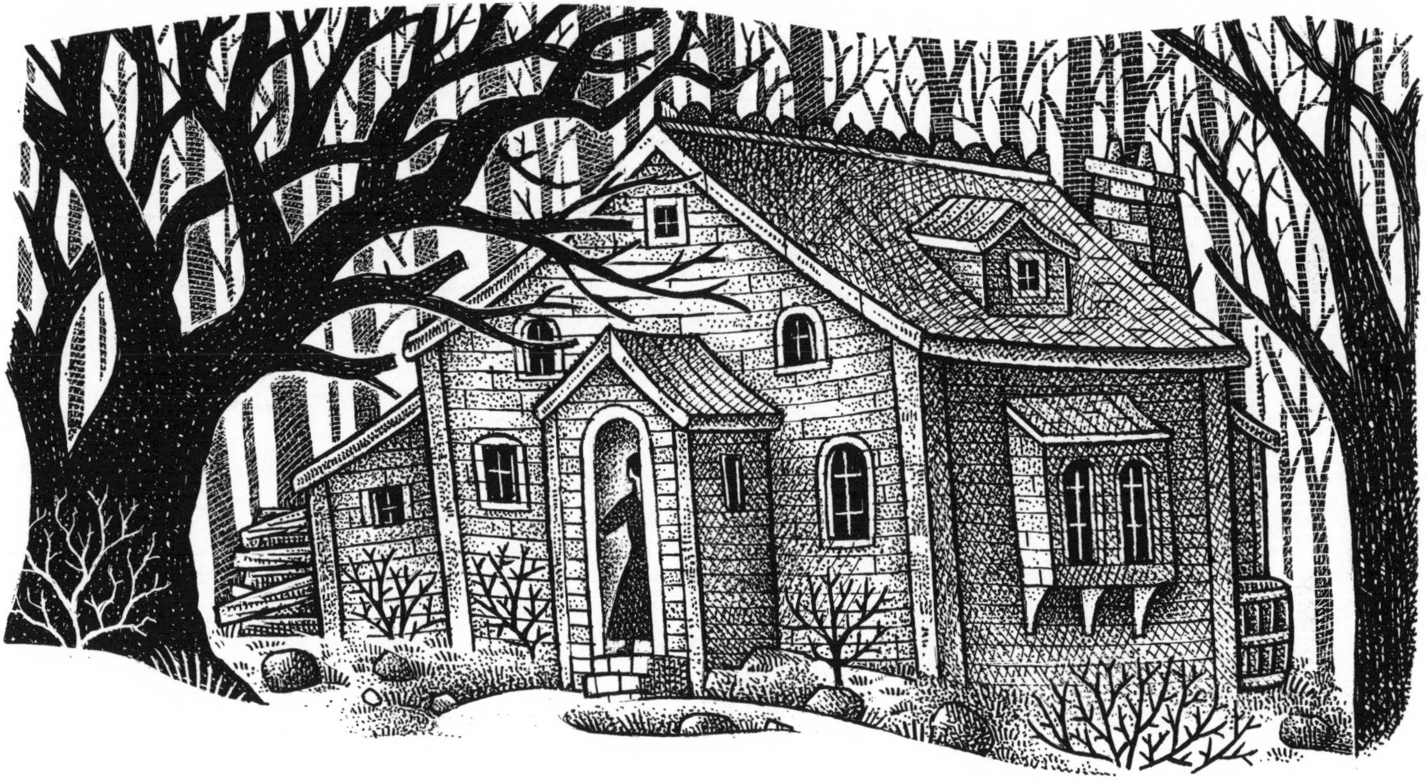

RIVAL WITCHES

was fighting with her rival witch, she had left him alone. Now she would renew her curse and ruin him. In despair he spoke to his wife about moving away while they still had some money saved. They agreed to put the business up for sale and move to her parents' hometown as soon as possible.

When the merchant got to town the next morning, however, he saw that Black Mag's mercantile was dark. He did not know what to make of this curious circumstance, given that the witch opened her store every day—even Sunday, when churchgoing businessmen took a day of rest. The sheriff was summoned to check on Black Mag; no one else was brave enough to go to the witch's house.

The sheriff found Black Mag lying on the bedroom floor, silent and still, with the poisoned beauty cream smeared across her face. She was dead.

Crouched on top of the dressing-table mirror was a large black raven, which stared at Black Mag with a malicious gleam in its beady eyes. The sheriff shivered, wondering how the carrion bird had gotten into the closed room and why it was sitting calmly on such a precarious perch rather than feasting upon the body of the witch. Opening the window, he shooed it outside.

As the raven departed with a rush of dark wings, it gave a hoarse cry that made goose bumps rise on the sheriff's arms. Within the bird's call he distinctly heard the triumphant laugh of Handsome Abbey.

35

The Birth of the Jersey Devil

THE PINE BARRENS

Something inside Mother Leeds snapped when she found out she was pregnant yet again, this time with number thirteen. Life was already a struggle with an unreliable and sometimes abusive husband and twelve little children to feed. She worked hard, so very hard, to keep food in her children's stomachs and clothing on their backs. She had not yet managed to put shoes on every foot, but perhaps this last batch of sewing she'd taken in would buy another pair.

Her husband drank away the little money he earned when he felt like working, and more often than not, lately, he did not feel like working at all. A lazy husband might be bearable, for Mother Leeds had enough gumption for two. But the combination of lazy and abusive was not. She spent all the time she wasn't working keeping her children (and herself) away from her husband's ill temper. She had no family and no one to turn to for help, so she remained with her husband and endured.

When her husband arrived home from the tavern in Burlington that evening, Mother Leeds gave him the news with all the gumption and fire she'd had when they first met, before life had become so unbearably hard.

"A curse be on you," she shouted at him fiercely, "for your indolence and your sloth and your abusive ways! May a curse be on this child, too. May it be a devil to plague you for your sins!"

When Father Leeds raised his hand to her, she ducked under his fist and thrust him out the door with both hands. He fell head over heels, too drunk to catch himself, and landed in the water trough.

"This child will be a devil!" Mother Leeds shouted again, so loudly that the entire neighborhood could hear. "Thirteenth child! Devil's child. And it will come for you first."

Mother Leeds was terrible in her wrath. Her dark eyes blazed almost red in the dim light of the rising thunderstorm. Her arms were spread wide as if she were cursing the whole world, rather than just her good-for-nothing husband. Her children cowered in the back room watching their parents. As Mother Leeds pronounced her curse, a sudden lightning bolt seared a tall pine tree at the edge of the clearing where their small house stood, and a thunderclap shook the house and ground.

She stood unmoving during the burning crash, her long, tangled hair lifting crazily about her wild-eyed figure in the electrified air following the lightning bolt. Father Leeds gave a shout of terror, leapt from the water trough, and fled from the clearing, never to be seen again in the Pinelands.

Mother Leeds went back into her house, as calm as if nothing had happened, and sent her children to bed. All that night and all the next day a terrible storm raged over the Pinelands, flooding the rivers and tearing trees from the ground. But Mother Leeds was serene as she fed the children and sewed the shirts she'd promised to deliver to the local store.

"Will the baby really be a devil, Mama?" her eldest son asked her timidly after a particularly loud thunderclap.

"Yes, my son," she replied calmly. "And you must take your brothers and sisters far away when it is born, or you will suffer the same fate as your father."

The children didn't believe her, of course, but word of the terrible curse swiftly made its way through town and countryside. Folks were hesitant to have any dealings with Mother Leeds, afraid that she might be a witch, but some of the local women stood up for her, knowing what kind of life her husband had given her. The minister spoke to her a few times, asking her if she had any sins she wished to confess to him, but she just smiled calmly, placing a hand on her expanding middle, and said no.

Two months before her thirteenth child was due to be born, Mother Leeds began making arrangements for her children. She secured apprenticeships for the elder boys and housemaid jobs for the older girls. A week before the baby was due, she sent her three youngest children to stay with their eldest sister, who had recently married a local farmer and set up housekeeping in a nearby town.

A storm was raging the night that Mother Leeds was brought to bed in childbirth. The room was full of local women. They had gathered to help her, more out of curiosity than good will, having heard the rumors that Mother Leeds was involved in witchcraft and had sworn she would give birth to a devil. No one believed it, of course, for Mother Leeds still went to church every Sunday, and no harm had come to her when she spoke with the minister. Still, they were curious.

Tension mounted when the baby finally arrived. It was a relief (and to some a disappointment) when the baby was born completely normal. The midwife cleaned the child and swaddled him in a warm blanket. Turning to hand him to Mother Leeds, she abruptly screamed and dropped the bundle on the floor. The women gasped in horror, but Mother Leeds just watched patiently, knowing what was to come.

The bundle on the floor jerked and writhed, and suddenly the child burst forth from the blanket, changing before their very eyes. He grew larger and larger, hands and feet transforming into claws, wings erupting from his shoulder blades, horns sprouting from his head, and dark eyes glowing with yellow fire like the eyes of a cat. Within minutes, the child was completely grown. Mother Leeds stared in satisfaction at her child, who now resembled a dragon with a head like a horse, the body of a snake, a forked tail, and the wings of a bat.

The more intelligent of the women had taken to their heels the minute the bundle started writhing. Those who remained, horrified and fascinated by the spectacle, immediately got a beating as the devil child's thick forked tail and two enormous wings thrashed about. Even Mother Leeds was not spared a pummeling as she staggered weakly from the bed, still bloody from giving birth. Slowly, she gestured to the chimney.

"You know what you must do," she gasped to the creature.

With a harsh cry, the Leeds Devil flew up the large chimney and vanished into the storm. Lightning struck the blackened stump of pine tree in the same place it had struck the night that Father Leeds had vanished from the Pinelands. A huge clap of thunder shook the house and ground.

THE BIRTH OF THE JERSEY DEVIL

When the women had recovered enough from their fear to look around the room, Mother Leeds lay dead beside the chimney. There was a look of peace on her face that the women in the room did not share, for they knew that she had unleashed a Devil upon them all.

They say, though no one knows for sure, that Father Leeds was the first victim of the Jersey Devil. Several of the Leeds children also disappeared in the course of the next few months—those who had not listened to their mother and had taken local jobs rather than leaving the town where they grew up.

Long after all the Leeds family had passed on, the Leeds monster—called the Jersey Devil—continued to haunt the Pinelands of New Jersey, wreaking havoc upon farmers' crops and livestock, poisoning pools and creeks, and appearing on the Jersey shore just before a ship wrecked.

36

A Devilish Kind of Week

CAMDEN

Sunday, January 17, 1909

It all started on an ordinary Sunday in January. It was colder than a witch's heart outside, so I was glad to be manning the desk at the police station. I was doing all the nitpicky paperwork Uncle Sam deems necessary when in walked trouble. He was wearing the uniform of an on-duty patrol officer and his expression was one of fear mixed with glee. It was one of the new officers, a young chap, still green around the gills. He scampered about my desk, as excited as a chipmunk in a grove of walnut trees.

"Sir! Sir! He's been spotted!"

"Who's been spotted?" I asked calmly, fingering my .38 with the meditative air I used to squash the brash younger set.

"The Jersey Devil!" The new officer practically shouted the name in his excitement.

"The Jersey Devil, you say?" I replied, leaning back in my chair and putting both my feet up on the desk. "Tall horned chap, thick neck, short front legs, longer legs at the rear, glowing eyes, strong pair of wings, forked tail, goes by the name of Leeds?"

"That's him! That's him!" yelped the officer with the enthusiasm of a pet Yorkie given a steak. "A patrolman making the rounds of Buckley Street over in Bristol, PA, saw him last night. Shot at the monster a few times, but the Devil just flew away. The officer said he had a scream that chilled the blood!"

"Sounds like the patrolman has spent one too many evenings on night duty," I said casually. "Are you sure the slugs he was packing were bullets and not bourbon?"

"He swears it's the truth!" the young man replied. "And there have been other sightings as well."

"Do tell," I invited, knowing I was going to hear about them anyway.

According to my officer's source, the postmaster of Bristol had also seen the Jersey Devil. He had watched the creature flying low across the river. Another fellow named Owen had seen a "strange creature that had a screech like an upset infant" near the canal.

The young officer chattered enthusiastically about strange tracks that were found in Bristol and Burlington. *So, the creature has returned to its native soil,* I mused as he described some muskrat trappers who had tracked the large, hoofed creature for a mile through the snow, and a Gloucester City liveryman who found the Devil's footprints in eight different yards, including McHugh's junkyard. As the officer yapped to a close, I sighed inwardly. The newspapers were going to be full of this.

After the officer left my desk, I considered the facts about the Jersey Devil. The trouble had begun with a dame, of course. Somehow it always did. This particular dame was known as Mother Leeds. Rumors circulated that she was involved in witchcraft. Moreover, she was expecting her thirteenth child—not a good number. The dame had sworn that she would give birth to a devil, and that is exactly what she did.

It was a traditional dark and stormy night in 1735 when Mother Leeds was brought to bed in childbirth. The room was full of womenfolk gathered to help her, more out of curiosity than goodwill. After all, they had heard the rumors about Mother Leeds and didn't want to be left out of the excitement. Tension mounted until at last the baby arrived. It was a relief (and to some a disappointment) that the infant was born completely normal. Then, before their terrified eyes, the child began to transform. The room erupted with screams as he grew at an enormous rate, becoming taller than a man and changing into a beast that resembled a dragon, with a horse's head, a snake's body, and a bat's wings. As soon as it was fully grown, the monster began beating the women (including its mother) with its thick, forked tail. Moments later it flew through the chimney and vanished into the storm, leaving only a harsh cry as evidence of its presence.

After that the Jersey Devil regularly haunted the Pinelands, committing all sorts of misdemeanors: killing farmers' livestock, poisoning pools and creeks, disturbing the peace. In my opinion, they should have locked it up then and there, but no one knew how to catch the creature. Finally, some preacher took a bell, book, and candle and exorcized the devil, sending it away for good. At least that was the working theory. It was a good theory, too, until it was blown out of the water by a Pennsylvania policeman with a pistol.

I sighed. There was sure to be a ruckus. The newspapers would go to town on the story, and people would storm into the police office demanding protection; they always did when things got hot around Camden. I had my work cut out for me.

Monday, January 18

Mother Leeds's little darling was a busy boy during the next several hair-raising hours. The track-sightings in Burlington grew more frequent, and several unnamed folks were rumored to have actually seen the "Flying Death." People started barricading themselves into their homes. Those brave enough to go outside reported overturned garbage cans and tracks going from ground to tree to fence to rooftop to ground in an inexplicable manner. (Inexplicable, that is, unless you can fly.) I did not envy the Burlington police force its monumental task—keeping the peace.

Fear of the Devil spread like wildfire. By Monday night, reports were coming in from Columbus, Hedding, Kinkora, and many other rural communities in Burlington County. A posse formed in Jacksonville to hunt the creature, but the dogs refused to track it and the men involved claimed that the footprints disappeared after four miles. There was one amusing little report I received from Officer Stehr in which a local farmer, having set up a couple of steel traps on his property to capture the creature, managed to bag a Jersey Devil hunter instead.

I cut out a drawing of the Jersey Devil from a Philadelphia newspaper and tacked it to the wall, much to my colleagues' amusement. That was the last laugh we had. The next day, the Devil showed up on our turf.

Tuesday, January 19

The first report I heard Tuesday morning was from a Gloucester City family named Evans. Awakened by noises outside around

2:00 a.m., they went to the window and saw the Jersey Devil cavorting on top of their shed. Mr. Evans worked up enough nerve to open the window and yell "Shoo!" The Jersey Devil barked at him and departed with a flap of its large wings.

I was still pondering the report when an officer scrambled into the office shouting, "Sir! It's been here!"

I sat up sharply. "The Jersey Devil?" I exclaimed.

He nodded breathlessly. "Will Pine's daughter spotted the tracks on her way to deliver his lunch pail. Fainted dead away, poor kid!"

I leapt to my feet. Now it was serious; now the creature had come into my territory without so much as a by-your-leave. "Show me!" I commanded.

The patrolman led me to the site. Will Pine was there, guarding the tracks. I examined them carefully. They looked like they belonged to a two-footed donkey, with one foot slightly larger than the other.

Before I could surmise anything else, we were summoned to Dialogue's Shipyard to see another set of tracks. On our way, a trembling chap stopped us, claiming that he had seen the Jersey Devil right in the city. He told us that the creature was the size of a large dog but resembled a possum with wings. It had barked shrilly at the man before flapping away. He swore on a stack of Bibles that it was the truth.

I was feeling pretty grim by the time I returned to the office. I could see it already in the city streets—people shying nervously at sudden sounds and hurrying to their destinations. The people in my city were afraid, and I didn't like it. Not at all. One of my men showed me the latest sketch of the Jersey Devil from the late edition of the *Philadelphia Evening Bulletin*. As he hung it beside our rapidly growing art gallery, my only comment was, "They made the hooves too large." But inwardly, all I could think was, *Just you stay away from my town.*

Wednesday, January 20

Wednesday was pretty calm around Camden, meaning that we had no Jersey Devil sightings. But stories kept rolling in from outside the city. An officer in Burlington saw the Devil and reported that its eyes blazed like coals, but it had no teeth. *No teeth,* I mused. *Then why the dickens are people afraid of it?*

A posse led by Station Agent Kirkwood in Collingsworth managed to get close enough to spook the creature. They caught a glimpse of it flying north toward Moorestown, where it appeared near the Mount Carmel Cemetery. A brave resident chased it until it disappeared into a flooded gravel pit—a favorite spot for local anglers. The Jersey Devil sped past a peacefully fishing man, who was understandably upset by the encounter.

In Riverside an officer investigating the reported killing of a young pup discovered strange tracks around its body and on the roof of a nearby house. When the same tracks appeared in the backyard of Justice Ziegler, who had ordered the investigation into the dog's death, the enterprising judge immediately had plaster casts made and put them on display in his office. Both the pup's demise and the prints in Ziegler's yard were attributed to the Jersey Devil.

The last sighting on Wednesday was by a trolley car operator passing through Springside late in the evening. He got the shock of his life when his headlights picked up a strange "winged kangaroo" that zipped across the tracks and disappeared into the shadows.

Thursday, January 21

After the Springside episode, I was afraid to go home in case something happened closer to Camden. I kept my officers on their regular shifts to ensure that everyone got some sleep, but we were all on high alert. So we were ready when a report came in. The Black Hawk Social Club had been holding its regular meeting on Ferry Avenue right here in Camden when the Jersey Devil appeared at the window. The members had stampeded out of the building while one Mr. Rouh had bravely threatened the beast with a club, causing it to fly away with a bloodcurdling shriek.

Around 2:00 a.m. the Jersey Devil accosted a trolley headed for Camden. It had just passed through Haddon Heights when the winged terror was spotted by passengers, who crowded to the windows. As the trolley halted to pick up another rider, the Jersey Devil flew overhead, hissing and circling the trolley menacingly before sailing away. According to reports, it then alighted on the road to Trenton, where it spooked a horse and carriage. When the driver got down to see what was causing his horses to rear and lunge, he found himself face to face with the monster, which hissed at him, beat its wings, and flew away.

Throughout the day on Thursday, additional reports—along with much coffee—were brought into my office. We heard about dead chickens, hoofprints, eerie cries, and several more encounters throughout the area. Councilman R. L. Campbell of Clayton even submitted an erroneous report of the creature's death. A railroad track worker claimed that he saw the Jersey Devil sniffing the third rail when its forked tail lashed out and touched it, causing an explosion. Fire and smoke billowed everywhere, and the track was burned out for twenty feet on either side of the accident. The worker was sure that the Jersey Devil was dead, though no body was found.

That report was soon nullified by sightings in Beaver Pond, Philadelphia, Westville, and West Collingswood. In the latter, the Jersey Devil alighted on the roof of a shed at the fire chief's home. Two firemen spotted it and turned in an alarm that brought the whole crew out. They aimed a hose at the beast, which prompted it to flap down the road a bit. But before it flew away, the Jersey Devil turned and charged the firemen, scattering everyone.

Then it returned to my turf. At 7:00 p.m. the Jersey Devil made its way up Mount Ephraim Avenue to the home of one Mrs. Sorbinski, of South Camden. Hearing a commotion in her yard, the brave lady hurried outside with a broom in hand. She was concerned for the safety of her dog—and with good reason. The pet, which had been left outside, was in the claws of the Jersey Devil. Mrs. Sorbinski flailed at the Devil with her broom. Immediately, it released the dog and flew right at her. At the last second, it veered away and sailed over the fence.

Mrs. Sorbinski screamed in panic and shock as she carried her dog indoors and phoned for help. Patrolmen Crouch and Cunningham were dispatched to the house. As they strove to calm Mrs. Sorbinski and the gathered neighbors, they heard piercing screeches from the standpipe in Kaighn Hill. The officers ran to the location and emptied their revolvers in vain at the creature silhouetted against the night sky. It soon flew away into the darkness.

I was only minutes behind the patrolmen, but I did not arrive in time to see the beast that was making my life—and all the lives in my city—miserable. We ordered everyone home. The streets of Camden, usually bustling even at night, were empty.

Friday, January 22

In the wee hours of the morning (around 2:00 a.m.), the Stenburgs, who lived at the corner of Ferry Street, had a visit from the Jersey Devil. Mrs. Stenburg heard the creature alight on the roof and shook her husband awake. He grabbed a rifle but did not manage to get a shot off before the beast flew away.

I was in my office at 4:00 a.m., drinking coffee and trying to stay awake, when Officer Stehr burst into the station. He was shaking with nerves. "A jabberwock!" he shouted. "I saw it drinking from the horse trough in front of John Carroll's saloon."

This was it! I knew it in my bones. I had to calm down my officer first, so I played it cool.

"A jabberwock, eh?" I replied, leaning forward and raising an eyebrow. "Tall horned chap, thick neck, short front legs, longer legs at the rear, glowing eyes, strong pair of wings, forked tail?"

"That's it," Officer Stehr said, obviously relieved that I believed his story.

"You said it was at Carroll's saloon on Third Street," I repeated, rising slowly from my desk.

Stehr took one look at my face and backed away. "Right. On Third Street," he stammered.

I'd had enough. The Jersey Devil had appeared one too many times on my turf, and it was going to pay. I grabbed my rifle and stomped out of the office.

"What are you going to do?" Officer Stehr shouted after me.

"I'm going to clean up this mess once and for all," I roared and ordered him to man the desk. I stalked into the town, my rifle over my shoulder, and headed to Third Street. I found the Devil's tracks easily enough and followed them. I took my time. This was between me and the Jersey Devil, and the fewer people to observe the showdown, the better.

The tracks ended in a field outside town. It looked as if the beast had flown up into the trees. I squinted in the predawn light, looking around me. And there it was, a tall horned creature with a thick neck, short front legs, longer legs at the rear, glowing eyes, wings like a bat, and a forked tail.

"Get down here and fight like a man," I bellowed, shaking my fist. The Jersey Devil studied me thoughtfully for a moment and then swooped right over my head and landed in the field behind me. It probably expected me to duck and flee, but I was too angry to do more than curse when its hooves almost brushed my hair. I whirled to face it and sighted along my rifle.

"You're under arrest for disturbing the peace, assaulting an officer, and scaring the dickens out of half the residents in Camden," I said, moving slowly toward the creature. "There will be more charges as soon as I can think of them."

The Jersey Devil seemed to think that we were playing a game. It lowered its horned head a little and started toward me, imitating my slow, deliberate walk. I considered the matter as we confronted one another. This creature supposedly could blow fire—at least that's what they were saying down in Philadelphia, although there was nothing to confirm that report. It had touched the third rail on the railroad tracks and lived to tell the tale, and bullets didn't seem to faze it. Not good. That meant my rifle was probably useless. Unless . . .

I began to grin. To my knowledge, the Jersey Devil had run away from at least two encounters in which someone beat at it:

Mr. Rouh had used a club, Mrs. Sorbinski a broom. I fingered my rifle thoughtfully.

I paused less than three feet from the monster. It paused, too, raising its wings, showing its teeth, and doing a strange little dance. Obviously the Jersey Devil was trying to intimidate me. Well, I meant to intimidate it right back into the Pine Barrens for good. I hissed at the creature and then started to roar in the voice that made all the men under my command turn yellow and creep out of the station. The Jersey Devil flinched. Raising my rifle, I brought the butt down onto the beast's nose. It gave a shriek of shock and back-winged. I hit it on either side of the head with the barrel, shouting and cursing. The Jersey Devil began to howl, and I howled back as I kept on beating it with my rifle. As it stumbled backward, trying to escape from me, I let off a series of rifle shots right in its ear. The sound was deafening. The Jersey Devil clamped its small forelegs over its ears and whimpered.

"Now get out, and don't ever show your face here again," I whispered into the ear of the cowering creature and gave it a kick in the hind leg to convince it of the serious nature of my request. I backed off just enough to give it some room to cock its wings. The creature crouched and then sprang into the air, wings beating. It flew away frantically, looking over its shoulder once to make sure I wasn't pursuing it. I waved my rifle a final time as it zoomed over the horizon toward Pennsylvania. I didn't care where it went, so long as it made itself scarce on my turf.

I went back to the office and sent Stehr home to recover from his encounter with the "jabberwock." Then I spent the rest of Friday reassuring Mrs. Sorbinski and many other good people

A DEVILISH KIND OF WEEK

in Camden that the Jersey Devil was gone. I had personally taken care of the matter, I told them, though I did not explain further. The citizens were only somewhat comforted. Many still refused to come out of their houses, and the theater was forced to cancel its performance that evening. But over the next few weeks, the hysteria died down and life returned to normal.

Looking back now, I wonder why the Jersey Devil stirred from its home in the Pine Barrens. I may never know—but if anyone wants to know how to get rid of the Devil, I would be happy to supply them with the answer.

37

Nine Eleven

HOBOKEN

As a special treat for our twentieth anniversary, we decided to take the sunset cruise around lower Manhattan the Sunday before Labor Day. It was a silly thing to do—totally tourist— but sometimes playing tourist is fun, even for someone living and working daily in the shadow of the Big Apple. My husband took me out for a fancy lunch at a restaurant near the South Street Seaport, and we lingered over linguine for more than an hour before the boarding call came.

The ship was packed with tourists from all nations, wearing sunglasses and talking in half a dozen languages. But the smiles and gestures were universal. Everyone was amazed by the Statue of Liberty and Ellis Island, and by the glow of the sunlight on the towering New York skyline.

My husband nipped down to the concessionaire and returned with two cups of hot chocolate, just perfect for sipping in the cool breeze that whipped around us as the boat moved through the choppy water.

My husband was all over the place with his digital camera, taking photos of everything from a seagull perched cheekily on a rotting dock to the grinning tour guide as he pointed out

NINE ELEVEN

the sights. Finding me leaning against a rail, watching lower Manhattan glow with golden light as the sun set in the west, he took my hand and gave me a kiss. "Happy twentieth anniversary, sweetheart," he murmured in my ear and gave me a tickle and a squeeze. I squealed like a teenager and then hugged him back. He put his camera away, and we stood watching as dusk crept over the city and one by one the lights came on. That was glorious, too.

We were on the East River now, between Brooklyn and lower Manhattan. Muttering something about catching the reflections on the water, my husband grabbed his camera and hastened to the front of the boat. I watched him go with a grin. Twenty years of marriage had hardly changed him! Well, five minutes of romance was better than none, I decided with a shake of my head and a fond smile.

I returned my gaze to the beautiful glow of the World Trade Center, its twin towers looming over the rest of the city like matching sentinels. Then I blinked suddenly in surprise as the whole world shivered around me. A keening noise sounded in my ears, as if a high-pitched alarm was going off or someone was blowing a dog whistle. The air started to shimmer before my eyes, like heat rising from pavement. And then I was looking at the harsh white light of midmorning in New York City and, before me, the silhouette of a large jet airliner was flying straight toward the North Tower of the World Trade Center! I gasped and shouted an idiotic warning to the pilot, who could not possibly have heard me from a boat on the East River. My garbled words came out as a tiny squeak, which was lost immediately in the wind. A moment later, the airplane intersected with the tower and disappeared.

My heart was pounding painfully against my ribs as I leaned hard against the rail, hyperventilating in alarm. My hands gripped the bar so hard that my knuckles were white with the strain. What had just happened? Knees trembling, I stared in shock as morning sunshine lit the World Trade Center, wondering where the airplane had gone. Had the pilot swerved at the last minute?

Suddenly a second silhouette—also of a large airplane—appeared from the opposite direction and flew straight toward the South Tower. I thought I would faint as it intersected with the shimmering building and vanished. The keening sound rose higher in pitch until my ears burned with it, and tears sprang to my eyes. Goose bumps covered my whole body as the air twisted and writhed around me. For a moment, I smelled smoke and heard screams. A tight, too-calm voice said, "Nine eleven. Nine eleven." It sounded like a cry for help. Or a prayer.

Yes, I thought fuzzily, *someone should call 9-1-1.* If ever there was an emergency, this was it.

And then the world shuddered back into its proper place. I was staring at two glowing towers in the gentle light of sunset, and the voices of happy tourists murmured all around me. A young couple turned to me with excited smiles and asked me to take their picture with the World Trade Center in the background. I accepted the camera with shaking hands and had difficulty lining up the shot for them. I kept expecting the silhouetted airplanes to fly into the towers and ruin the picture. I was certain the tourists would find the pictures too blurry to keep when they reviewed them later.

I was still shivering when my husband returned and casually slung his arm around me. Turning away from the magnificent glitter of lights on the horizon, he asked: "Are you cold, honey? Do you need your sweater?"

"I'm fine," I said shortly, not wanting to explain the strange vision I'd seen. I couldn't understand it, and I didn't want to think about it.

"Wow, look at that," my husband cried, pointing upriver. Thrusting away the strange appearance of two silhouetted planes flying right into the twin towers, I obediently gazed upriver and drifted back into tourist mode.

A few days later, I was vacuuming the living room after breakfast when the phone rang. It was my husband, calling from his office in midtown Manhattan. "Turn on the television right now," he said, knowing I rarely watched TV in the morning. His voice sounded strange. I grabbed the remote control and switched on the television. Immediately, the screen was filled with a picture of the World Trade Center towers, black smoke billowing up around them.

"Two planes just hit the towers," my husband said, as the newscaster's voice told me the same thing. "I can see the smoke from my office window!"

I gasped in shock, my heart seeming to pause inside my chest, and I nearly dropped the phone. Two airplanes . . .

Oh . . . my . . . God!

Two airplanes had hit the twin towers.

I fell to my knees, body shaking so hard I couldn't stand. I heard my husband's voice in the phone. It sounded a long way off, as if he lived on another planet.

"Honey, did you hear me? Honey?"

Hearing alarm in his voice, I put the receiver to my mouth and gasped, "I heard you. I'm watching it now."

I put the phone back down, just as the scene on the TV cut to a clip of the second plane hitting the South Tower. I shut my eyes in extreme mental agony. It was exactly the scene I'd seen in silhouette during our Labor Day cruise around New York City.

My husband was talking again. I opened my eyes and tried to pick up the phone. It kept slipping out of my sweating hands. After three tries, I leaned down and spoke into it, reassuring him that I was all right—at least physically.

We stayed on the phone together, watching our separate newscasts as rescuers tried to get to the people trapped on the upper floors of the two burning towers, listening to panicked newscasters speculating as to the cause of the disaster.

My husband and his colleagues had gathered in a meeting room with a window overlooking downtown Manhattan. They were simultaneously watching the newscast on television and looking out the window at the chaotic scene. I could hear bits and pieces of their commentary as I stared at my own TV screen. Once, I heard my husband exclaim in horror as he witnessed several people throw themselves off the top of the twin towers to avoid burning to death in the fire that encased the upper floors.

There came an unexpected rumbling sound. People began screaming and shouting on the television as first one and then the second tower collapsed before my stunned gaze. My heart squeezed with pain. *What about all those people trapped inside?* I thought in horror. I realized that I had just seen hundreds of real people with real lives die in an instant.

My stomach roiled. I ran for the bathroom and was sick into the toilet. Twice. I sat beside the bowl, panting and wiping the sour taste from my mouth, too sick to stand up. I was horrified beyond even tears, my body shaking. *Dear God,* I prayed, and stopped, not knowing what else to say.

Suddenly, I flashed back to my Labor Day vision. Oh, my gosh—had my vision somehow caused this? My body shuddered in fearful reaction to the thought. But no—how could it? I'd seen a vision of this disaster, what my Nova Scotian grandmother called a forerunner. But I'd never heard of visions *creating* disasters. I hoped.

This is not your fault, I told myself firmly.

I hauled myself upright, using the toilet as a crutch. I rinsed the bitter taste from my mouth and brushed my teeth. Then I walked shakily to the living room, one hand on the wall for support, and sat down on the couch to watch events unfold in New York City, my mind stunned into a strange stillness that was probably shock. A small voice in the back of my brain started speculating on how many of my friends—or my friends' friends—worked in the World Trade Center. And how many of them had made it out alive.

I don't know how long I sat on the couch, unable to move, unable to look away from the chaos I saw on the TV screen. My thoughts came slowly, one at a time, as if they were swimming through cold molasses. Where would these terrible events take us as a nation? This day felt momentous, life-changing in some negative way.

What day is it, anyway? I wondered abruptly. As if in answer, I heard the newscaster say in a tight, too-calm voice, "We will never forget the events of this day, September 11, 2001."

I took a deep breath and burst into tears. It was September 11. Nine eleven.

38

The Clown Mannequin

SOMERSET COUNTY

Jan arrived promptly at 6:45 p.m. for her babysitting job. The Smiths lived in a rambling old farmhouse set in the middle of a fenced-in yard. Rhododendrons lined one side of the house, and Rose of Sharon bushes dominated the other. In front was an overgrown English garden, and in back was a large lawn perfect for football games. Jan loved the Smiths' house. She hoped to own a place like this someday, when she was a rich and famous author. But for now, Jan appreciated the chance to hang out in such a lovely house with two rambunctious but enjoyable twin boys.

Normally the boys and their Yorkshire terrier, Lady, came spilling out the front door when Jan arrived. Tonight, Jan found herself walking to the front door of the old house unaccompanied. This was highly suspicious. Mrs. Smith opened the front door with a smile and greeting. A moment later, two syrupy-sweet voices called to Jan from upstairs, "Jan! Come up and look at our comic book collection." This was extremely suspicious behavior. Mrs. Smith gave her a meaningful grimace that confirmed Jan's theory: The Smith boys were up to something.

Jan carefully climbed the stairs and walked down the hall, expecting the boys to jump out at her any second. Nothing happened. She knocked on the twins' bedroom door. "Come in," the boys called. Jan swung the door open warily and found herself facing a menacing six-foot-tall clown mannequin. It leered evilly at her through white-lashed red eyes, its large red grin painted so wide it nearly touched the too-large ears. A happy spotted hat bagged over one ear and matched the ludicrous red-spotted baggy pants, which were held up by red suspenders over a white shirt.

Jan shrieked in horror and stumbled backward out of the room. She tripped on the edge of the hall rug and sat down hard. Inside the bedroom, the twins laughed hysterically and their little Yorkie barked. The dog ran into the hall to frisk around the humiliated Jan as the twins rolled on the floor at the mannequin's feet.

"I told you she'd be frightened," cried Eddie.

"Say hi to our new friend," leered Freddie, grabbing the mannequin's shirt and walking it toward Jan.

"That thing is hideous," Jan said, pulling herself upright on the hall table. Her legs were shaking so badly she could hardly walk. "Why do you have such a hideous thing in your room? Clowns are creepy!"

"Hahaha," chortled Freddie. "Clowns are creepy!" He thrust the mannequin's hand toward Jan. "How do you do?" he asked in a fake deep voice.

"Ugh," Jan said, avoiding the mannequin's hand. Close up, she could see the elastic band that attached the clown mask to the mannequin's head. "I don't know how you can stand to keep such a creepy thing in your room! I will be downstairs if you twin nightmares need me!"

Jan stalked out of the room and slammed the door behind her. That mannequin was truly horrible. There was something so eerie about a clown. You could never tell what they were thinking behind the makeup. Ugh!

Downstairs, Mrs. Smith was looking for her glasses and Mr. Smith was adjusting his tie, using the stainless-steel refrigerator as a looking glass.

"You have our cell-phone number?" Mrs. Smith said. "And the number of the police station? And you know to call 9-1-1 if there is a fire or some emergency?"

Jan grinned. Mrs. Smith always ran through this litany before going out. Jan solemnly assured her that she knew what to do in an emergency.

"The Dantes are home tonight," Mrs. Smith continued, gesturing to the blue ranch house next door. "You can always run over there for help if there's a fire."

"There won't be a fire," Mr. Smith said, smoothing down his rather crooked tie. "Don't worry, Martha."

"I've heard there's an escaped convict on the loose in the next county," Mrs. Smith continued, ignoring her husband. "That serial killer who killed all those children in Virginia. So be sure to lock the doors behind us."

"Martha, you are going to scare Jan so bad she won't babysit for us again," Mr. Smith complained. "Come on. We are going to be late for our dinner reservation."

Mrs. Smith called the twins downstairs to kiss them good-bye and asked them to set the table for Jan. As she breezed out the back door, she called, "Dinner is in the oven. And remember to lock up behind us."

Jan hurried around the house, locking all the doors. Between the creepy clown mannequin upstairs and Mrs. Smith's talk of an escaped serial killer, she wasn't taking any chances.

Once she was done locking up, she pulled a casserole out of the oven, and everyone sat down at the table to eat dinner. Lady begged winsomely beside the twins' chairs until they caved in and gave her a bite from their plates. The Yorkie was trotting purposefully toward Jan when her head went up and she stopped to listen. A moment later, she bounded out of the kitchen and ran upstairs. Jan heard her barking at something in the twins' room. Then she heard a thud and the barking stopped abruptly. "What was that? Is something wrong?" she asked the twins.

"Nah," said Freddie. "Lady likes to bark at the squirrels in the oak tree outside our window."

"She jumps on the bed and throws herself at the glass," Eddie added, spooning more casserole onto his plate. "Sometimes she knocks her head so hard she gets dizzy and has to lie down. Silly dog."

The little Yorkie was still upstairs when the twins and Jan finished dinner. "I'm pretty full. How about we wait for a few minutes to eat our ice cream?" Jan suggested.

The twins clutched their full stomachs and agreed.

"Let's run upstairs and check on Lady," Jan said. "Then we can watch your favorite TV show. It starts at eight."

The twins cheered at both these suggestions. They charged upstairs and burst into their room, calling for Lady. Jan, jogging at their heels, reeled back a step or two when she saw the clown mannequin by the window. It was almost as much of a shock on the second viewing as it had been on the first.

Jan frowned suddenly. Something was different in here. Hadn't the clown mannequin been standing in the center of the room? The boys must have moved it after playing their practical joke on her.

On the far side of the room, the twins were kneeling on the floor, looking under the bunk beds for Lady.

"She's not in here. She must be downstairs in her basket," Eddie said. "Come on." He rushed away and Freddie followed. Jan cast one last shuddering glance at the clown mannequin before following the boys. For a moment, she thought she saw its chest move. And was that a blink? *Ridiculous,* she said to herself, goose bumps all over her body. *I hate clowns.* She hurried down the stairs, glad to get away from the creepy mannequin.

"Lady is in her basket in the laundry room," Freddie announced as Jan hurried into the front hall. "She's sleeping. She must have knocked her head really hard against the window."

Jan peeked in at Lady, who was curled up on the splotchy white cushion in her basket. There were wet paw prints leading toward the basket. Jan wondered if the washing machine was leaking. Before she could investigate, Eddie called to her from the living room, and she hurried to answer him. She'd check on Lady once the twins had settled down to watch their show.

In the kitchen, Jan scooped vanilla ice cream into two bowls. Then she went into the living room and handed the bowls to the twins, who were already absorbed in their cartoon. Freddie looked up suddenly and said, "Jan, I forgot to bring my bike in from the yard, and it's supposed to rain tonight. Would you please get it for me?"

Jan gave the tousle-haired boy a mock frown. "After the scare you gave me with that clown, I should make you do it!"

Freddie clasped his hands in supplication and gave her a cherubic grin. Jan relented. "All right, you monster. Watch your show. I'll be right back, so don't eat all the ice cream!"

Jan jogged out through the back door and glanced around the yard. No bike. Freddie must have left it on the side of the house. She circled the premises clockwise until she saw Freddie's bike lying between the oak tree and the rhododendrons. As she picked up the bike, she glimpsed a funny-shaped clump lying in the bushes under the twins' window. Jan wheeled the bike over to take a look.

Something about the huddled shape made Jan's skin feel clammy and her knees shake. It resembled a human body. But that was nonsense! Jan had to force herself to take a closer look. To her horror, Jan saw a naked mannequin lying under the bushes, stripped of its gaudy clothing and clown mask. Chills ran through her body at the sight. Dear God. If the mannequin was down here, than what—or *who*—was upstairs in the boys' bedroom?

Panicked, Jan dropped Freddie's bike and sprinted frantically for the back door and the TV-watching twins. The vision of the too-still form of Lady lying in the basket replayed itself in her mind. She'd wondered about the funny splotches on the white cushion. They'd looked like splotches of blood. And wet paw prints on the floor leading to the basket. *Dear God, don't let me be too late!*

Jan spun around the corner into the living room and stopped in heartfelt relief. The boys were still sitting on the couch, absorbed in their cartoon. They looked up in surprise at her sudden entrance. Putting her finger to her lips, Jan beckoned mysteriously to them, hoping their curiosity would overcome their desire to watch TV. Eddie and Freddie glanced questioningly at her. They opened their mouths to speak, but she shook her head and beckoned again. Silently, the boys came over to Jan, who caught each of them by an arm and hustled them out the back door and over to the neighbor's house without explanation. Once the twins were safe with the Dantes, Jan dialed 9-1-1 and begged the police to send someone over to check the house. Then she called the Smiths and told them to come home at once.

"I am probably being silly," she said to Mrs. Dante. "But I'm sure it was the twins' mannequin lying in the bushes, yet I saw the clown mannequin upstairs!"

An unmarked police car pulled into the driveway, and Jan ran to meet it so she could explain what she'd seen in the twins' room. The police officers sent her back to the Dantes' home to wait while they checked the house. The Smiths arrived, and Jan was trying to explain to the frantic parents the reason she'd called the police when gunshots exploded upstairs. Jan screamed as a man in a clown costume plunged backward through the twin's bedroom window, glass shattering everywhere. The man hit the ground with a loud thud and lay still at the base of the rhododendrons as more police officers drove up to the house. In the flashing red and blue lights cast by the police cars, Jan could see that the dead clown had landed right beside the body of the mannequin that he had replaced in the bedroom.

Much later, the police told Jan and the Smith family that the escaped serial killer had climbed the oak tree, crept into the twins' bedroom, and disguised himself as a clown, throwing the

THE CLOWN MANNEQUIN

incriminating mannequin into the bushes where it wouldn't be seen. He had slit the little Yorkie's throat when she barked at him, and the poor mite had crept downstairs to bleed to death in her basket while the killer waited upstairs for the twins' bedtime. If Jan had not seen the mannequin when she went outside to pick up Freddie's bike, the boys and Jan would have been murdered.

39

Buckeye

LAMBERTVILLE

It was November 1935 and the big football game was right around the corner: New Hope Buckeyes versus Lambertville Eagles. The teams were archrivals and this was their moment of glory. Only one team would walk away in triumph, and Lambertville was determined to be the one on top.

The week leading up to the game was full of hostility, both covert and overt. Students mocked each other whenever their paths crossed. Nasty practical jokes were played in the name of school spirit. A group of New Hope parents had a screaming match with one of the coaches after practice. Emotions ran so high that the police were prepared to increase their presence in the area during the game.

There was an unspoken reason behind the increased tension this year, and her name was Marie. She was a new student at Lambertville High School, and she was as pretty as the day is long. She was also an incorrigible flirt and was toying with the hearts of two boys. Not just any two boys, mind you, but two star football players—one from Lambertville and one from New Hope.

Marie liked to tease her two beaus about one another, making first one then the other green-eyed with jealousy. It created a lot of tension between the schools, already bitter rivals, and the tension grew worse as the big game drew near.

The night before the game, the two boys came face to face at a local diner. The restaurant got real quiet as each boy measured the other up. Members of both football teams arranged themselves behind their representative, ready to fight. The manager of the diner had the telephone in his hand, ready to call the police, when the Lambertville boy spoke: "Whoever wins tomorrow's game gets the girl. Deal, Buckeye?"

The New Hope boy nodded grimly: "Deal, Eagle-boy. It will be as easy as stealing candy from a baby."

The Lambertville boy gave him a twisted smile: "Keep telling yourself that, Buckeye. 'Til tomorrow."

Just like that, the two teams dispersed and the manager slowly hung up the phone, wondering what the morrow would bring.

Word of the agreement moved swiftly through both towns. Every seat was filled in the stands as the Lambertville students burst forth from their prep rally, banners streaming, to face the New Hope Buckeyes, who'd arrived by bus a few minutes before.

The first quarter of the game was tense as the teams moved swiftly up and down the field without scoring. A few fistfights broke out in the stands, and at least one parent was hauled off the field after shouting obscenities at the Lambertville coach.

Marie sat demurely in the stands, watching her rival beaus trying to outperform one another on the football field. Brilliant throws, showy catches, strong tackles—the boys were playing their hearts out.

By halftime the score was tied 21–21. The halftime show went by in a blur. Everyone was waiting with baited breath to see which team would win the game, which boy would win the girl.

At the beginning of the third quarter, the New Hope boy made a spectacular catch and raced down the field toward the end zone, pursued by a good third of the Lambertville team. New Hope fans screamed themselves hoarse with excitement, and Lambertville fans screamed with outrage. Then the Lambertville boys overwhelmed the wide receiver, and he went down under a pile of bodies.

When the Lambertville team rose in triumph, the New Hope boy stayed prone on the field. The look of triumph died from the Lambertville team as they gazed down on their rival. The boy's head was twisted almost completely around, and he was not breathing. Slowly, the team backed away as coaches, parents, and medical personnel swarmed the field. But there was nothing they could do. The boy's neck was broken. He was dead.

The football game was forfeited and the two teams trudged from the field, rivalry temporarily put aside in their shock and grief. This was not the way football games were supposed to end. Marie pushed her Lambertville beau away, sobbing in remorse. It was only when she saw her New Hope beau fall beneath a pile of bodies that she realized which boy she really loved. Too late.

In response to a petition from the dead boy's family, New Hope disbanded its football team due to the danger of the game. And Lambertville lost its greatest rival.

After the New Hope boy's death, folks grew uneasy if they had to cross the Lambertville football field after dark. Some claimed they felt the spirit of the Buckeye boy lingering in the vicinity, still determined to win Marie away from his rival. Others saw a pair of red eyes in the woods behind the goalposts.

Lambertville High School closed its doors in 1955, and the abandoned building became a haunt of gangs from several of the local towns. One night a gang from Lambertville descended on the old building around sunset. They sat drinking on the steps as their leader related the story about the Buckeye who died for love on the football field. At the close of the story, the newest gang member, who was still trying to prove his worth to the other fellows, staggered to his feet and raised his drink mockingly toward the old football field. "That's cheating, Buckeye!" he shouted. "Lambertville would have won the game if you hadn't cheated. I challenge you to a race across the football field. The best man gets the girl!"

The boys laughed uproariously at this challenge. But their laughter was muted by a sudden cold wind that blew across the football field and swirled around the steps where they sat. The smell of decay and death filled their nostrils, and the boys' hearts pounded in sudden fear. On the far side of the darkened field, two red lights—like a pair of evil eyes—appeared among the trees. Then an eerie voice spoke, its icy tones reaching down through each pair of ears and twanging their nerve endings like too-tight strings: "I will race you, Eagle-boy. Run across the field from end to end, or die like me!"

The Lambertville boy shot to his feet as if under a spell. "No," he gasped. "No!" But his legs were already propelling him toward the football field. "Help me!" he cried to his friends

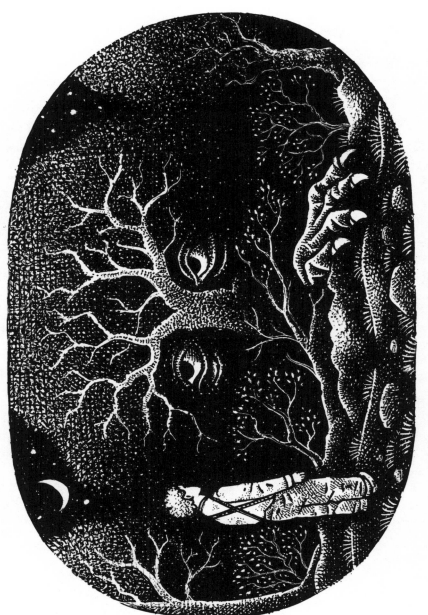

as his body took control over his mind and pushed him into a gallop across the field.

The panicked Lambertville gang hustled to their feet and raced after him. None of them wanted to run toward the glowing red eyes, but none of them wanted to be left alone at the abandoned school either, not after hearing that icy voice. They pounded across the field as fast as they could and then veered under the goalpost and raced toward the car, wanting to get away from the haunted football field as fast as possible.

It was only when the boys were halfway home that they realized that two of their number were missing. None of them dared go back to see what had happened to them.

In the morning, the bodies of two Lambertville boys were discovered up at the abandoned high school. Both of their necks were broken and their heads were twisted almost completely around, in the manner of the dead New Hope football player. One of the dead boys was the new Lambertville gang member that issued the challenge to the ghost.

40

The Leather Purse

MORRISTOWN

I never knew quite what it was about the old leather purse that so fascinated my grandmother. It was an ugly thing made of some strange kind of leather with a mark on the back of it that looked like a tattoo. Grandma kept it in a special display case in her living room. Her house was old and smelled of dust and mildew most of the time. I didn't like visiting it.

Now don't get me wrong. Grandma was okay as far as adults go. She always had molasses cookies fresh-baked for me and Mama when we came for our weekly visit. And I loved playing in her big backyard with the rope swing and the basketball hoop. But the inside of her dusty old house always felt a little macabre, a little strange. And the strangeness seemed to center around the funny leather purse in her display case.

When I was twelve, Grandma asked me to stay with her sick dog while she ran errands. The poor golden retriever needed medicine every couple of hours, so someone had to watch him. His dog bed was in the kitchen, which was good since I had no intention of going anywhere else in the creepy old house until Grandma came back.

I'd just finished giving the dog his dose of medicine when I heard an angry thumping sound coming from the living room. I froze in the act of putting the spoon in the sink. I was alone in the house, I thought. My skin was all-over goose bumps. Was a burglar trying to break in?

I glanced over at Grandma's golden retriever, expecting him to bark at the sound. He just sighed and rolled over, as if strange crashes from the living room were a normal thing. Not a burglar then.

Cautiously I grabbed a big rolling pin out of the drawer and went to investigate the sound. I tiptoed down the hallway and peeked through the living room door. A man was standing in front of the display case. He was dressed in strange old-fashioned clothes like a person from a historical television program, and he was glaring at the weird leather purse. My heart thudded with fear at the sight of the stranger. I clapped a hand over my mouth to stifle a gasp and started to back away.

As if he sensed my presence, the man turned around to glare maliciously at me. He took a step forward and I screamed. I couldn't help myself. Immediately the man vanished into thin air. I screamed again, realizing I'd just seen a ghost in my Grandma's creepy old living room.

My grandmother had returned while I was investigating the thumping noise. I heard the back door slam, and Grandma rushed into the hallway just as I was rushing out. We collided and almost fell over the plant stand. She then rocked me in her arms as I sobbed out the story.

"Oh honey, I am sorry you saw that," Grandma said. "That's just old Antoine LeBlanc trying to get his skin back."

This explanation made me feel worse, not better.

"Trying to get his skin back?" I shrieked, causing the golden retriever to rush into the hallway, barking madly.

"Didn't your Mama tell you the story of Antoine LeBlanc?" Grandma asked in surprise. "Everyone knew it back in my day. Maybe she thought it was too gruesome for you to hear when you were little."

Grandma sat me down at the kitchen table and gave me a glass of milk and a molasses cookie. Then she told me about Antoine LeBlanc.

LeBlanc was the son of a wealthy family in France who came to American expecting to take up a fancy position as the overseer of a large estate. Instead, he found himself employed as a simple gardener by the Sayer family of Morristown. Angry and disillusioned, LeBlanc tolerated his change in status for one week before he viciously murdered Mr. and Mrs. Sayer and their servant girl and stole away with a pillowcase full of money, jewelry, and silverware.

Fate was obviously stacked against the murderous LeBlanc, for the pillowcase came apart at the seams as he was fleeing the scene. Silverware and money spilled out onto the roadway, marking his departure. The next morning a Sayer family friend found some of the monogrammed silverware in the road and brought it to the local police. The police went to the Sayer home and found the three murder victims. The evidence at the scene pointed to the new gardener as the chief suspect, so the authorities went looking for LeBlanc. They found him in a tavern in Hackensack.

LeBlanc was taken to jail, where he confessed to the crime. A jury found him guilty of murder, and he was hanged before an angry crowd of bystanders. Instead of burying the corpse, the body was given to a local surgeon for dissection and for use in his science experiments.

Being of an enterprising nature, the sheriff also ordered the body skinned and the murderer's hide tanned. Souvenirs such as leather wallets, book covers, lampshades, and handbags were created from LeBlanc's leather hide and were sold to anyone who wanted a memento of the murderer's comeuppance.

My eyes got really big as I realized what Grandma was saying. That leather purse in her display case must be one of the relics of the murderer, made out of his skin. Someone in Grandma's family had purchased it as a grisly souvenir after LeBlanc's hanging and passed it down to her.

I totally lost it. I lurched from the chair and vomited on the floor. No wonder Grandma's house always felt so macabre to me. She had a murderer's skin on display in her living room! Everyone at school said that ghosts couldn't rest until all of their body parts were together. So LeBlanc's spirit was haunting my grandmother's house, trying to retrieve the strange leather purse with the tattoo on the back. A tattoo, I realized, that was once on LeBlanc's body!

I vomited again, right on top of the poor golden retriever, and ran from the house. Grandma called something after me, sounding almost as distressed as I felt, but I refused to look back at her. I was never going into that house again.

Mama was furious with Grandma for a long time after this incident. I was sick with a fear-induced fever for almost a week after seeing the ghost, and I refused to go anywhere near my grandmother or her house. It was only after Grandma telephoned to say that she'd disposed of the leather purse that we reconciled with her.

I was in my mid-twenties when Grandma died. Mama had also passed unexpectedly in a car accident the year before, so I was the sole executor of Grandma's estate. It was a hot July day and I was sorting through all the junk in her rented storage unit when a cold breeze washed over my skin. I had just picked up a beat-up old hatbox, and I glanced around in surprise when the temperature dropped so suddenly. Standing in the doorway of the storage unit was a dark-haired, dark-eyed man wearing the clothes of a nineteenth-century workman. I recognized him at once. It was the ghost of Antoine LeBlanc.

I knew immediately what must be under the lid of the battered old hatbox. It was the old leather purse made from his skin. Grandma hadn't disposed of the artifact—she'd just removed it from her house so that Mama and I would resume our weekly visits.

I gave a squeak of terror and dropped the hatbox. The top fell off, and the leather purse rolled across the floor and landed at the feet of the ghost. LeBlanc gave a wordless shout of triumph and snatched it up in his hands. There was a blinding flash of light and the ghost was gone, just like that.

The employee who was monitoring the storage units came charging out of the office and rushed over to the unit where I stood trembling from head to toe. "There was a huge electrical surge down here," the man exclaimed. "All of the computers crashed. Were you hurt? I saw the flash from my office and I was afraid you might have been electrocuted."

"I'm all right," I gasped, collapsing onto the nearest box. I immediately disproved this assertion by bursting into tears. The poor man didn't know if he should get me a tissue or call

THE LEATHER PURSE

an ambulance. I pulled myself together pretty quickly, all things considered, and wiped my eyes on my sleeve.

I asked the employee to throw the hatbox away for me. I couldn't bear to touch it. Then I locked the storage unit and went home. In the morning I intended to call my favorite charity and donate everything in the storage unit to their cause, with the caveat that they had to clean the unit out themselves. I didn't care what Grandma kept in there. Everything in that storage unit was tainted in my mind by the presence of that terrible leather purse. Let the charity have whatever money came from the sale of those objects. I was done with all of it—and with Antoine LeBlanc. This time for good.

Resources

Adams, Charles J., III. *Atlantic County Ghost Stories*. Reading, PA: Exeter House Books, 2003.

———. *Cape May Ghost Stories*. Vol. 2. Reading, PA: Exeter House Books, 2003.

Asfar, Daniel, and Edrick Thay. *Ghost Stories of America*. Edmonton, AB, Canada: Ghost House Books, 2001.

Beck, Henry Charlton. *The Roads of Home: Lanes and Legends of New Jersey*. New Brunswick, NJ: Rutgers University Press, 1995.

———. *Tales and Towns of Northern New Jersey*. New Brunswick, NJ: Rutgers University Press, 1964.

Botkin, B. A., ed. *A Treasury of American Folklore*. New York: Crown Publishers, 1944.

———. *A Treasury of Railroad Folklore*. New York: Crown Publishers, 1953.

Brunvand, Jan Harold. *The Choking Doberman and Other Urban Legends*. New York: W. W. Norton, 1984.

———. *The Vanishing Hitchhiker*. New York: W. W. Norton, 1981.

Coffin, Tristam P., and Hennig Cohen, eds. *Folklore in America*. New York: Doubleday and AMP, 1966.

———. *Folklore from the Working Folk of America*. New York: Doubleday, 1973.

Cohen, Daniel, and Susan Cohen. *Hauntings & Horrors*. New York: Dutton Children's Books, 2002.

Cohen, David Steven. *The Folklore and Folklife of New Jersey*. New Brunswick, NJ: Rutgers University Press, 1983.

Dorson, R. M. *America in Legend*. New York: Pantheon Books, 1973.

Editors of Life. *The Life Treasury of American Folklore*. New York: Time, 1961.

Erdoes, Richard, and Alfonso Ortiz. *American Indian Myths and Legends*. New York: Pantheon Books, 1984.

Flanagan, J. T., and A. P. Hudson. *The American Folk Reader*. New York: A.S. Barnes, 1958.

Hauck, Dennis William. *Haunted Places: The National Directory*. New York: Penguin Books, 1994.

Holub, Joan. *The Haunted States of America*. New York: Aladdin Paperbacks, 2001.

Homer, Larona. *The Shore Ghosts and Other Stories of New Jersey*. Wallingford, PA: Middle Atlantic Press, 1981.

Hufford, Mary T. *Chaseworld*. Philadelphia: University of Pennsylvania Press, 1992.

Leach, Maria. *The Rainbow Book of American Folk Tales and Legends*. New York: World Publishing Company, 1958.

Leeming, David, and Jake Page. *Myths, Legends & Folktales of America*. New York: Oxford University Press, 1999.

Macken, Lynda Lee. *Ghosts of the Garden State*. Forked River, NJ: Black Cat Press, 2001.

———. *Ghosts of the Garden State II*. Forked River, NJ: Black Cat Press, 2003.

———. *Ghosts of the Jersey Shore*. Forked River, NJ: Black Cat Press, 2011.

———. *Ghosts of the Jersey Shore II*. Forked River, NJ: Black Cat Press, 2014.

———. *Haunted Cape May*. Forked River, NJ: Black Cat Press, 2002.

Martinelli, Patricia A., and Charles A. Stansfield Jr. *Big Book of New Jersey Ghost Stories*. Mechanicsburg, PA: Stackpole Books, 2013.

———. *Haunted New Jersey*. Mechanicsburg, PA: Stackpole Books, 2004.

McCloy, James F., and Ray Miller Jr. *The Jersey Devil: 13th Child*. Moorestown, NJ: Middle Atlantic Press, 1976.

Moran, Mark, and Mark Sceurman. *Weird N.J.: Your Travel Guide to New Jersey's Local Legends and Best Kept Secrets*. New York: Barnes & Noble, 2003.

———. *Weird N.J. Vol. 2: Your Travel Guide to New Jersey's Local Legends and Best Kept Secrets*. New York: Sterling, 2006.

Mott, A. S. *Ghost Stories of New Jersey.* Auburn, WA: Lone Pine Publishing International, 2006.

Okonowicz, Ed. *In the Vestibule: True Ghost Stories from the Delmarva Peninsula to the Jersey Shore.* Vol. 4. Elkton, MD: Myst and Lace Publishers, 1996.

Peck, Catherine, ed. *A Treasury of North American Folk Tales.* New York: W. W. Norton, 1998.

Pierce, Arthur D. *Iron in the Pines.* New Brunswick, NJ: Rutgers University Press, 1957.

Pitkin, David J. *Ghosts of the Northeast.* New York: Aurora Publications, 2002.

Polley, Jane, ed. *American Folklore and Legend.* New York: Reader's Digest Association, 1978.

Reevy, Tony. *Ghost Train!* Lynchburg, VA: TLC Publishing, 1998.

Schwartz, Alvin. *Scary Stories to Tell in the Dark.* New York: Harper Collins, 1981.

Seibold, David J., and Charles J. Adams III. *Legends of Long Beach Island.* Reading, PA: Exeter House Books, 1985.

Skinner, Charles M. *American Myths and Legends.* Vol. 1. Philadelphia: J. B. Lippincott, 1903.

———. *Myths and Legends of Our Own Land.* Vol. 2. Philadelphia: J. B. Lippincott, 1896.

Spence, Lewis. *North American Indians: Myths and Legends Series.* London: Bracken Books, 1985.

Stansfield, Charles A., Jr. *Haunted Jersey Shore.* Mechanicsburg, PA: Stackpole Books, 2006.

Zeitlin, Steven J., Amy J. Kotkin, and Holly Cutting Baker. *A Celebration of American Family Folklore.* New York: Pantheon Books, 1982.

Zimmerman, Linda. *Ghost Investigator: New York & New Jersey.* Vol. 4. New York: Spirited Books, 2004.

Zwillenberg, Elias. *New Jersey Haunts.* Atglen, PA: Schiffer Publishing, 2010.

About the Author

S. E. Schlosser has been telling stories since she was a child, when games of "let's pretend" quickly built themselves into full-length tales acted out with friends. A graduate of Houghton College, the Institute of Children's Literature, and Rutgers University, she created and maintains the award-winning website Americanfolklore.net, where she shares a wealth of stories from all fifty states, some dating back to the origins of America. Sandy spends much of her time answering questions from visitors to the site. Many of her favorite e-mails come from other folklorists who delight in practicing the old tradition of who can tell the tallest tale.

About the Illustrator

Artist Paul Hoffman trained in painting and printmaking. His first extensive illustration work on assignment was in Egypt, drawing ancient wall reliefs for the University of Chicago. His work graces books of many genres—including, children's titles, textbooks, short story collections, natural history volumes, and numerous cookbooks. For *Spooky New Jersey*, he employed a scratchboard technique and an active imagination.